bitter

alexina anatole

a cookbook

T0333026

SQUARE PEG

bitter

In memory of my two favourite Campari drinkers: Grandpa and Robert

portrait photography
danika magdelena

food photography
yuki sugiura

food styling
lola milne

prop styling
susie clegg

cover
evi-o.studio

book design
studio 7:15

contents

finding the beauty in bitterness

introduction

Where does your mind go to when I mention the word 'bitter'? Maybe you find yourself wincing – or perhaps your mouth puckers in anticipation. Whether referring to food or emotions, bitterness is broadly considered an undesirable trait. But I feel for bitterness: it's hard for him to win against his rivals in the world of taste. Sweetness is all butter-wouldn't-melt, saltiness is powerful, sourness is fun – and umami, well, he's the popular kid these days. Is it any surprise that bitterness gets picked last for the team?

But I'm here to change that. I didn't repeatedly cook with bitter flavours on *MasterChef* to challenge people – I did it because I love the complexity, depth, dimension and nuance that bitterness adds to meals. It stimulates the appetite, has the ability to boost other flavours, balances out meals that could be considered too fatty or overly sweet, and that's before we consider all the amazing health-giving properties that innately bitter ingredients hold. We should all be showing bitterness just as much love as we show the other four tastes. And while a contingent of our society might claim to dislike bitterness, some of the most widely popular foods on this planet are characteristically bitter: coffee, cocoa, beer, walnuts . . . I could (and will) go on. In John Torode's words: 'This is the dangerous world that Alexina likes to live in.' Welcome!

This cookbook will explore bitterness – where it appears, how to use bitter flavours in your cooking and why they're good for us. I look at 10 classic bitter ingredients in detail with a broad selection of more than 80 recipes, from weeknight meals to desserts and weekend projects to impress, from gluten-free and vegan to fish and meat dishes. In short, this book will show you how bitterness can be beautiful.

what is bitterness?

Bitterness is enigmatic. It's often confused with sourness or umami, or defined by what it isn't: 'a lack of sweetness' . . . it's hard to pin down. But when I reflect on bitterness – which, alongside salty, sweet, sour and umami, is one of the five basic tastes – the most honest way that I can describe it is as a hard, unpleasant edge . . . a confrontation. When you eat something that's a little (or a lot) bitter, you sit momentarily on a fine border between pleasure and disgust.

One of the best ways I've seen the effect of bitterness demonstrated is in a film that documents a range of children experiencing their very first tastes of certain foods. In it, a young girl tries a bitter, salty olive. The initial reaction is unmistakably one of disgust: her face screws up, all the muscles in her body are held in tension and she looks as if she'd like to do nothing more than spit the olive out immediately. But something starts to happen a few seconds in: her face relaxes a bit, curiosity flashes across her features. Then her arms start to lift, a smile twitches at the corner of her mouth and, before we know it, she is grinning. What initially seemed unpleasant has become enjoyable on some level: she has warmed up to the flavour. *What is that all about?* I suppose writing this book is my quest to understand this exact reaction.

I appreciate that describing bitterness as 'a hard, unpleasant edge' isn't starting things off on a positive note, but let's be real: bitterness is typically the least popular of the five tastes. And its prolonged association with poison hardly helps: our ability to detect bitterness is widely believed to have been born of a need to protect ourselves from consuming toxic plants and substances. The truth is that while not all bitter foods are toxic, most toxic foods are bitter. And yet, weirdly, many bitter foods are labelled 'superfoods' these days (looking at you, kale) due to their high levels of antioxidants. Such inconsistencies beg the question: when is bitterness a defect and when is it an asset?

We don't have to worry about the link between bitterness and toxicity anymore because we are no longer required to forage unknown, wild foods for our dinner. In fact, eating bitter foods – if the ingredients highlighted in this book are any indication – is overwhelmingly something you *should be* doing. Throughout the chapters in this book, I tackle the specific health properties of grapefruit and bitter oranges, bitter leaves, tahini, beer, walnuts, cranberries, tea, coffee, cocoa and liquorice. In doing so, I have noticed a pattern: ingredients with strong, pronounced, complex flavours – i.e. most bitter ingredients – appear to contain more chemical compounds. What that means in practice is more antioxidants, more vitamins, more of the good stuff. And when you consult the history books, bitter ingredients and foods have long been celebrated across all the major civilisations for their health properties: Mesopotamian, Egyptian, Roman, ancient Chinese, ancient Greek, Mesoamerican. This is unlikely to be a coincidence.

But beyond health, there is flavour. Just as there are contradictions in the health credentials of bitter ingredients, so are there some in the flavour department, too. Bitterness is not a one-dimensional sensation and just because you like one bitter ingredient, it doesn't mean you'll like them all. While there is a single type of receptor on our tongues that registers sweetness, there are twenty-six receptors for bitterness, all of which respond to different bitter compounds. So, the fragrant bitterness of grapefruit – which runs very close to sourness – is different to the earthy bitterness of beer, which is distinct from the nicotine bitterness of walnuts. It is entirely feasible that you could love coffee but hate radicchio. The moral of this story? Don't be too quick to write bitterness off!

the death of my sweet tooth

Growing up, I didn't love bitter things – I'm not sure anyone does – but my journey with bitterness started in my late teens. Like many teenagers, I was desperate to be perceived as grown-up, and that meant enjoying (or appearing to enjoy) adult vices such as alcohol and coffee. Curiously, I approached these two bitter drinks in entirely opposite ways: with alcohol I forced down the hard stuff, while with coffee I eased myself in via sickly sweet white chocolate mochas from Starbucks.

As a child I would binge on sweet things. Initially it was British supermarket treats such as flap-jacks and mini muffins, but attending a mixed state school in south London exposed me to the sweetest of sweet things: boxes of syrup-drenched *gulab jamun*, trays of sticky Turkish *baklava*, plates of cinnamon-scented Portuguese *pastéis de nata*. I could eat several of these sugary enchantments in one sitting. Later, my sugar obsession transitioned to boxes of French macarons, which landed at university each term, addressed to me by generous relatives. In short: I was always transfixed by something sweet.

That sweet tooth eventually led me to the patisseries of Paris. I moved there after university, determined to work for Pierre Hermé, whose macarons I had coveted for years. Well, I can confidently tell you that one way to counteract a sweet tooth is to overdose. After months of consuming the many broken, unsellable macarons that resulted from the normal course of business – not to mention getting carried away at the product tastings that periodically took place at the atelier – I discovered the wonder of salt! Suddenly it wasn't the *petit gateaux* in the windows of the French patisseries that delighted me, it was the perfect baguette from the local boulangerie, slathered in intensely salty Normandy butter. To boot, I discovered 'the dark stuff' – bitter chocolate. My palate changed and life was never the same.

These days, I often start my day with half a grapefruit and will scoff the odd square of 85% dark chocolate when those afternoon cravings take hold. I like to buy a stick of liquorice from my local deli to chew on while I'm doing my weekend shop. Every winter, I stuff my freezer full of cranberries. Tahini dressing is the one I turn to more than any other. I am more than partial to a Negroni. If bitterness is an acquired taste, then consider it acquired around these parts.

bitterness:
the underdog

In some ways, I feel that we are increasingly gravitating towards bitterness: our growing love affair with dark chocolate, espressos and Negronis would suggest so, as would broader changes in the food space. The increased interest in umami, its sister trend fermentation, and all things charred, barbecued or burnt would seem to indicate a broadening of our collective palate. As does our appreciation for spice and chilli which can – like bitterness – border on the unpleasant. Arguably, we're now looking for flavours that move beyond the safe.

At the same time, I can't help but wonder: have we been gradually breeding bitterness out of our food? Is the fact that I no longer add sugar to my grapefruit in the morning a product of my changing palate or has the grapefruit itself changed? When I started writing this book I felt certain that the greens – salad, dark, leafy and otherwise – that we buy in supermarkets have become more tame. More people seem to love Brussels sprouts now and that can't simply be because we've learned that they taste good when cooked with bacon (or butter and garlic). Is it possible that the huge supply chains that govern a lot of how and what we eat might have decided to steer things in a more neutral, less challenging direction?

As it turns out, my instinct can be backed up by research. In 2015, scientist Marta Zaraska published a piece in *New Scientist* about precisely this phenomenon – and why it is so concerning. Since the 1990s, manufacturers have been seeking to make our foods – fruit and veg in particular – less bitter by removing the phytonutrients that result in this flavour profile. Unfortunately, in one foul swoop (pun intended) they are also removing the very chemicals that make these foods good for us. And so, a few questions remain: what are the long-term implications for our palates and our health? And is the current fashion for a Negroni down to our increasing appreciation for bitterness or simply compensation for the fact that we're being starved of this taste in our day-to-day diets?

It's hard to say. What I am sure of – it's why I have written this book – is that bitterness deserves its place at the table. As a taste, it is bracing, stimulating, surprising and strong – and when balanced properly, it contributes hugely to the moreish-ness of food. Bitterness is dangerous yet healthy; repellent yet addictive (think: alcohol, coffee, nicotine); grounding yet unusual. It is a contradiction and a bit of an enigma. But this is what makes it exciting and if I achieve anything with this book, I'd like to prove to you that, sometimes, the things that can seem unpleasant initially can turn out to be just right for you.

taste vs flavour

'Taste' and 'flavour' are used interchangeably and, mostly, that's fine. But it's still important to clarify that they are different: taste is a component of flavour, while flavour is the *whole picture*.

Taste refers solely to the bitter/sour/salty/sweet/umami qualities of an ingredient – i.e. what our taste buds, the mushroom-like receptors on our tongues, can distinguish. If we were to suck on a lemon, and then eat a passionfruit, our tongue would recognise both ingredients as sour, but it would not be able to distinguish between the two – even though they are not the same.

Enter flavour. Flavour is not just what the taste buds pick up on the tongue, but also what the olfactory system (our sense of smell) registers in the nose. The distinctions between different ingredients – what we mean when we talk about their flavour – are largely determined by aroma. Hundreds of volatile chemicals contribute to aroma, in thousands of combinations. The result? Endless flavour possibilities. But with so many options, it becomes hard to develop a useful vocabulary. The five tastes, on the other hand, are easier to grasp, so they form a good foundation for understanding flavour.

Finally, there is your palate: your individual ability to distinguish between and appreciate different flavours. Our sensitivity to bitter substances is determined in part by our genes, which code our specific set of taste buds. Some are 'supertasters' with more taste buds than average and greater sensitivity to tastes; some are 'taste blind' and relatively insensitive to stronger flavours. But exposure, life experiences and memories also play an important part in how we register flavour. Getting to understand how taste and flavour work in general, but also what your palate prefers, is essential.

flavour intensity

A general principle to bear in mind is that the combination of two different tastes (e.g. sweet and sour) is likely to result in something that registers as less intense on the tongue than if they were consumed individually, because they offset each other.

A natural example is a piece of fruit: an extremely underripe, sour peach has very little sugar (the sugar is stored as tasteless starch) and will cause your mouth to pucker up with the intensity of it. Equally, a mushy, overripe peach will have such a high sugar content that you might find it overwhelmingly sweet. A perfectly ripe peach, however, has both acidity and sweetness in balance so that you get the very best expression of that fruit's flavour: because no single taste dominates, you're fully able to absorb and experience all the aroma compounds that convey the wonders of that peach.

What's going on in that single piece of fruit is representative of what we want to achieve in our cooking. Making delicious food is, in part, about balancing the different tastes to create a flavour profile that is both exciting and harmonious.

Having said this, the way in which the five different tastes interact with one another varies according to what tastes you are pairing: the relationship between any two tastes is not always a balanced one. Sometimes one taste will dominate and the other might disappear, or merely fill the role of supporting act: an example being the way that certain sour ingredients, such as blackcurrant and lemon, have a remarkable ability to send the bitterness of coffee, chocolate and liquorice into the background. This will all become clearer as we dive into how bitterness specifically interacts with each of the five tastes.

understanding your palate

It would be incredibly neat to be able to give you a set of precise rules for how to combine tastes and flavours – but life is rarely that simple. Each of us is different, and so the way that we experience taste and flavour can vary, too. We do not all have the same sensitivities – what is hugely bitter for one person may not be very bitter for someone else. This is something to be celebrated, because it means that there is ultimately no right or wrong: there is only what *you* like.

In my supper clubs, I get a sense of how my guests' palates work depending on what courses they respond to most favourably. Those who adore a yuzu-based cocktail or green apple granita are clearly sour lovers; those who enjoy soy-braised short ribs favour salt and umami; and those who go mad for miso aubergine or vanilla custard are sweet fiends.

Getting to understand your own palate (as well as your family's and friends') will ultimately empower you to make subtle adjustments when cooking that result in something that is delicious to you (and whoever you're cooking for).

As an example: I tend towards sour and bitter, whereas my friend Jade veers towards sweet. So, when I shake us up a cocktail, I might add a little more lemon to mine, and a little more sugar syrup to Jade's – these subtle adjustments ensure that I get my ideal cocktail, and she gets hers.

Understanding your palate also makes it a lot easier to work out what cuisines you might appreciate most and what to order at restaurants – it's a form of getting to know yourself better.

how to handle bitterness

1 soooothe with dairy

2 balance with sweetness

3 distract with acidity

4 offset with salt

5 go all in, double down

1 soooothe with dairy

Food is comfort for many, and dairy is one of the most comforting (and delicious) food groups. Milk is the very first thing we consume as a baby and generally – though not always – dairy products are mild, smooth and soft. One of the most popular flavour combinations on this planet must be vanilla and cream (most typically combined in ice cream form) and you won't catch me arguing with the joy of this pairing. Still, to create a food combination that sends people wild, inviting bitterness to the party is a winner.

The Italians understand the power of combining dairy with bitterness and this is particularly evident in their desserts. We're not just talking about the Veneto region's infamous tiramisu here, but also the coffee granita served with softly whipped vanilla cream in the piazzas of Sicily; and Piedmontese *bônet*, where milk is balanced with cocoa and bitter local Fernet (a digestive herbal liqueur); and *affogato*, that perfect combination of vanilla ice cream with a shot of espresso. The simplicity of these desserts speaks to the power of bringing together dairy, bitterness and a little sweetness – no further embellishment required.

Savoury examples exist, too: the way that the Italians add bitter greens to ricotta to fill pasta, make *gnudi*, or top a *pizza bianca*; the milk that combines with bitter walnuts in *salsa di noci*; the combination of fresh, crunchy, bitter crudities with creamy, milky *bagna cauda*. And beyond Italy? The classic Belgian dish of chicory gratin (page 68), which pairs bitter chicory with milky béchamel sauce and plenty of cheese; the beer, milk and cheese that go into Welsh rarebit; the milk we add to our tea and coffee most days – not to mention the milk in our chocolate.

Science can help us understand why soothing bitterness with dairy is such a good tactic. Dairy is made up of protein and fat, and it is this combination which – when mixed with bitter flavour compounds – yields magic. Take a cappuccino as an example: when you combine bitter espresso with steamed milk, the proteins in the milk bind to the tannic phenolic compounds in the coffee, making these less available to our taste buds. As a result, the astringency of the coffee is reduced. The unfortunate side effect is that these proteins also bind to the aroma molecules, thereby weakening the overall flavour. But this is where fat comes in to save the day. Fat is a carrier of flavour: it helps to distribute seasonings throughout foods so that they make more contact with your tongue, resulting in greater depth of flavour. So, even as the proteins in dairy are hijacking some of the aroma molecules that would contribute to flavour via your sense of smell, the fat is ensuring that enough of the molecules that would be detected by your taste buds as sweet/salty/bitter/sour/umami remain. In short, fat, protein and bitter flavour compounds are perfect bedfellows.

So, remember: when it comes to bitter flavours, milk, cream and soft, mild cheeses such as mascarpone, ricotta and mozzarella – as well as creamy non-dairy options such as coconut milk – are your friends: they will happily mellow out bitter ingredients while still enabling their flavours to shine, allowing you to find an exciting balance between comfort and challenge.

Recipes to try:

Burrata, Radicchio and Olive Oil Breadcrumbs (page 60)

Tiramisu *Tres Leches* Cake (page 186)

Curry Leaf Mussels with Indian Lager (page 102)

2 balance with sweetness

There are several baking and dessert recipes in this cookbook where bitterness is a very welcome feature. Just as you often need a touch of sweetness to balance out a savoury dish with bitter flavours, you often need a sour or bitter element to cut through the sweetness in bakes and puddings.

There's not much of a chemical reaction happening between bitterness and sweetness: sugar doesn't interact with bitterness in the way that dairy or salt do (more on that next), but it does provide a flavour counterbalance that offers your taste buds some relief from too many bitter elements in your food. In fact, sweetness is effective at balancing out any of the other four tastes (for example, when you add a little sugar to a tomato sauce to bring the acidity into balance), so it is a helpful tool to use in the kitchen.

As a rule of thumb, wherever there is bitterness, you are likely to find sugar. With the exception of the 100% pure varieties, all chocolate contains sugar. Most coffee and tea drinks have additional milk, which is slightly sweet, if not the addition of sugar itself. Marmalade is a classic example of how we have taken the very bitter Seville orange and turned it into a well-loved feature of the breakfast table by adding mounds of white sugar. Similarly, in the Middle East, *halva* – in its basic form – is a combination of rich, softly bitter tahini with sweet honey (and occasionally a little more bitterness with the addition of cocoa). Even in Italian *amaro*, herbal digestifs, you find a combination of bitterness and sweetness. And from *amaro* to *amore*, I can't help but feel that – in both food and love – sweetness and bitterness make a perfect pair.

Recipes to try:

Raw Kale and Grapefruit Salad (page 64)

Cranberry and Pear Pie (page 150)

No-Churn Tahini Ice Cream with Caramelised Walnuts (page 94)

Scientifically speaking, this is the least reliable of the options because when you combine bitter and sour, three scenarios are possible:

1. The bitterness can enhance the sourness (which makes the sourness more dominant and the bitterness seem less as a result).

2. The sourness can suppress the bitterness.

3. If there's a lot of bitterness and sourness going on, they can mutually enhance each other.

Still, the effect I've noticed the most is that of sourness very effectively suppressing bitterness. The sourness of passionfruit cuts remarkably through the deep, bitter chocolate torte on page 204 and, for anyone who hates liquorice, you would be amazed at the extent to which the lemon cream neutralises the liquorice sugar that's tossed around the doughnuts on page 224 – a flavour combination I nabbed from the Swedes. Meanwhile, the sourness of pomegranate and bitterness of Campari seem to neutralise each other enough for the granita on page 54 to be palatable, although the complexity of flavour remains, ensuring it is an addictive combination.

I have also come to realise that when using an extra-virgin olive oil that has a degree of bitterness in a vinaigrette, the vinegar or lemon juice markedly reduces its bitter impact, while there might well be a reason that bitter leaves are so often paired with the acidity of lemon – either when cooked or in a dressing.

Perhaps this might also explain why grapefruit and cranberries, which are both bitter and sour, are often mistaken for being solely sour. The interaction between bitterness and sourness is an effect that certainly seems to be less recognised and talked about, but one that I am enjoying experimenting with.

Recipes to try:

Bitter Chocolate Torte with Passionfruit Sauce (page 204)

Liquorice and Lemon *Zeppole* Doughnuts (page 224)

Pomegranate and Campari Granita (page 54)

3 distract with acidity

4 offset with salt

Salty and bitter are both forceful tastes, and you might imagine that strong + strong would = stronger. But in reality, salt has a neutralising effect on bitterness. Whereas sugar simply offers a counterpoint to bitterness, salt has been scientifically proven to reduce bitterness to varying degrees by interacting with it (that said, it's a distinctly one-way relationship, as bitterness does not have the same effect on salinity).

Niki Segnit evocatively describes this effect in *The Flavour Thesaurus*: 'In Venice, in a bar in Campo Santa Margherita, you might try a *spritz al bitter*, which classically combines Prosecco, mineral water and Campari. After your first couple of sips, when you're wondering if you can take any more bitterness, a dish of green (salty) olives arrives and proves that you can.'

This relationship between salinity and bitterness explains the common practice of salting certain vegetables with a bitter edge – aubergine, bitter gourd – ahead of cooking. Likewise, Italians cook their bitter greens in well-salted water and then cover them in salty Parmesan. And without even going as far as to make a whole recipe, you can test this phenomenon for yourself: try a teaspoon of Campari or grapefruit juice as is, then take another teaspoon and add a pinch of salt before tasting – you'll be amazed at the difference. Similarly, a pinch of salt will effectively round out the bitterness of an espresso – try it!

Recipes to try:

Rarebit Mac'n'Cheese (page 106)

French Chicory, Roquefort and Walnut Salad (page 120)

Radicchio, Ricotta and Pancetta Rigatoni (page 72)

Bavette Steak with Chicory, Soy and Orange (page 70)

5 go all in, double down

Naturally, I subscribe to this approach – why be timid? And I am not alone: delicious examples abound of what I describe as 'bitter on bitter', in the form of G&Ts, Negronis, cigarettes and coffee, coffee and walnut cake, coffee and chocolate (mocha), brûléed grapefruit halves (caramel and grapefruit), Turkish coffee (cardamom and coffee) and so on. Of course, sweetness has a part to play in most of these combinations – but not all.

As with salt, it might seem counterintuitive that bitter on bitter would work, but sometimes two strong flavours offer the resistance that the other flavour requires to shine. When you pair bitter flavours, two things are going on: the first is that the bitter flavours complement one another since they are similar. The second is that the specific chemical compounds that contribute the bitterness in each case (let's call them 'bitter compounds') are likely to be different and thus have the potential to neutralise each other to some degree. The Negroni is a perfect illustration: you might not want to drink the individual components (gin, Campari, vermouth) separately – they would be too bitter and intense – but together? A sophisticated balance.

It's also worth mentioning that your palate does adjust to what you eat: just as with chilli heat, the more you eat bitter foods, the less sensitive you become. What's also true is that a large number of factors affect our perception of how things taste and, as we expand our taste experiences, we build associations and memories that start to mean more than our physical reaction to a particular flavour. Exposure, motivation and interest can significantly affect our tastes, so the more you double down on bitterness the more likely you are to develop a deeper love for bitter flavours. Think of doubling down on bitterness as the equivalent of immersion therapy for your taste buds.

Recipes to try:

Chicory Gratin (page 68)

Individual Negroni Pavlovas (page 50)

Cocoa Nib Tart (marmalade version) (page 202)

recipe list

breakfast + brunch

lunches, salads + sides

weeknight (veggie)

weeknight (fish/meat)

weekends + entertaining

baking

desserts

drinks etc.

salt

- Flaky sea salt has twice the volume of fine sea salt, so where a recipe asks for 1 tsp of flaky sea salt, you could substitute this with ½ tsp of fine sea salt if that's all you have (and vice versa).

- I like to use Diamond kosher salt for seasoning the water which I use to cook pasta, grains and vegetables, and to dry brine meat, as the salt crystals are fine enough to give an even coating and melt quickly.

- I tend not to use iodised salt as I find it has a chemical flavour.

dairy

- Eggs are UK medium, unless otherwise specified.

- Milk is always whole/full-fat, unless otherwise specified.

- Butter is slightly salted, unless otherwise specified.

baking

- Flour is plain (all-purpose) flour, unless otherwise specified.

- Sugar means either white caster (superfine) or white granulated sugar, unless otherwise specified.

- Where I specify 1 tsp vanilla bean paste, you could use ½ vanilla pod instead. I do not typically use vanilla essence or extract.

time

- I have come to realise that time is a key ingredient in the kitchen for two reasons:

    (1) it can allow flavours to deepen and harmonise;

    (2) it allows proteins (e.g. gluten, in eggs, etc.) to relax, which ultimately results in better texture.

- It's rare that a recommendation, for example, to rest a cheesecake overnight, *is* essential to a recipe working; but where such a recommendation is made, I promise you will be rewarded with a superior result for little (if any) extra effort.

- When it comes to timings in recipes, I have tried to offer some guidance, but I urge you to pay attention to the descriptive words and use your senses of sight, smell and hearing to glean when your onions are fully cooked, or your fritters are golden. Cooking is about developing and trusting your instincts.

grapefruit & bitter oranges

I'm not sure when or how, but at some point grapefruit became my brand. And I'm far from upset about this turn of events.

I love all citrus fruits, but grapefruit has a musky complexity that holds my interest: it is both sour *and* bitter (where most citrus is straightforwardly sour), which – for me – gives it an edge. Its distinctive but delicate flavour can be overwhelmed by too much heat, too much cream or too much sugar, making it hard to create delicious grapefruit bakes and desserts that retain the essential essence of the fruit. Still, I have made this my mission.

Once I started looking into the grapefruit's history, I discovered various nuances and oddities peppered throughout – and this only served to further convince me that the grapefruit and I are kin. All citrus originated from three species: the pomelo, the citron and the mandarin. Citrus fruits love to mate, which means that hundreds of varieties exist, most native to Asia. Grapefruit is the notable exception. Birthed in the Caribbean – Barbados specifically – in the early 1700s, it came about through the cross of an orange and a pomelo (which contributed its thick rind and slightly bitter-sour taste). Around the time that the grapefruit turned 100 years old, in the 1820s, Odet Philippe – a Black Frenchman who *loved* grapefruit – planted trees across Florida, which eventually started to produce red grapefruits (as opposed to yellow ones), and the well-known Ruby Red variety was born. In sum – given not only my Caribbean background, but an early childhood spent in France – the grapefruit and I share a degree of heritage.

It is rumoured that the grapefruit was known as 'the forbidden fruit' in the Caribbean. Whether this is true or not, it is an apt label for a fruit both complexly delicious and, as it turns out, legitimately deadly. When I started to talk about grapefruit more frequently, I received messages from thwarted grapefruit fans who informed me that while they would love to make my grapefruit cake/ice cream/hot sauce/dressing/insert-any-other-food-type-here, they simply couldn't because the grapefruit would interfere with their medication. It turns out that grapefruit has the power to increase the bioavailability of a host of drugs. This is because of anti-fungal compounds that grapefruits contain – have you ever noticed that they almost never go mouldy? Drugs are produced according to an assumption that the body will absorb only a limited amount into the bloodstream – let's say 10%. But absorption levels can jump significantly when certain drugs are consumed alongside grapefruit. Needless to say, this can be life-threatening. The key takeaway? Nature is all-powerful: man-made drugs are no match for the humble grapefruit.

In the West, grapefruits are most associated with breakfast: a ruby half covered in a rubble of sugar (brûléed, if you're somewhere fancy). However, grapefruit can feature in any course, because – as with most citrus – it works in savoury and sweet contexts. Often best raw, grapefruit likes other bold, unapologetic flavours: the aniseed notes of star anise, the bitterness of gin, the salty-umami hit of blue cheese. It is also great at cutting through rich things like fatty duck and luscious double cream. While I could never claim that the culinary possibilities with grapefruit are endless, they're certainly greater than you may have imagined. The unassuming grapefruit can usually be consumed year-round in the West (such is the privileged access we have to food these days), however they are at their peak at the beginning of the year: a true highlight in an otherwise thanklessly cold winter.

Seville oranges, meanwhile, are more extreme in their bitterness (and sourness) and their availability is limited strictly to January (your one opportunity each year to whip up a batch of very British marmalade). They have a thick, uneven, spongy peel and are cultivated mainly in Spain. In the UK, we reserve these bitter oranges primarily for marmalade, but the flower of the Seville orange tree also makes heady, evocative orange flower water, and the oil from their peel is used in orange liqueurs, such as Grand Marnier. In fact, my Iranian friend, Bobak, told me that every year his parents buy boxes of the fruit and use the juice in their cooking where they would typically use lemon. This makes sense given Iranians' propensity for sour flavours – and is perhaps an invitation for us all to experiment more with our use of these seasonal jewels.

winter citrus fruit salad

Serves 3-4

2 red grapefruits
3 oranges, preferably navel
100g (3½oz) seedless green grapes,
    halved or quartered lengthways
2-3 tsp orange blossom water (I use
    the Cortas brand)
½ tsp ground cinnamon

for the citrus sugar
1 tbsp caster (superfine) sugar
zest of ½ orange
zest of ¼ grapefruit

Fruit salad is often an afterthought, something we chuck into a breakfast spread or reluctantly make for dessert. It's certainly not something we tend to assign specific instructions to – it's supposed to be flexible! Easy! Accommodating! And I love the spirit of that, I really do. But if you thoughtlessly throw together a random combination of fruit – some in season, some not – and forget the 'dressing', then you will create something that is passable, but ultimately forgettable. We know that a little bit of thought and care can make all the difference to savoury salads; it's time to do the same for their sweet counterparts.

This fruit salad is beautiful, bright and cheering – perfect for enjoying in the dead of winter, when citrus fruits are at their best. Sweet oranges and grapes balance the more bitter, sour, complex grapefruit, and the addition of warming ground cinnamon and floral orange blossom water recall that classic Moroccan dessert of orange segments with cinnamon. Even better: unlike fruit salads made with fruits such as apples and pears, this holds up in taste, texture and colour over several days in the fridge. Eat as is, alongside thick strained yoghurt for breakfast, or with cinnamon-spiced French toast on the weekend.

I typically cut the citrus into segments, as explained below; however, for a brunch spread you might like to prepare the citrus fruit as shown in the photo for extra wow factor.

1.   Make the citrus sugar by placing the ingredients in a small bowl and rubbing the citrus zest into the sugar. Set aside. (Avoid making this too far in advance as it will crystallise.)

2.   Top and tail the grapefruits, then cut away the skin and pith from the flesh, allowing your knife to follow the contours of the fruit. Over a medium bowl, carefully cut between the membranes to release the grapefruit segments and let them fall into the bowl. Once you've removed the segments, squeeze what's left of the pith over the bowl to extract any remaining juice and then discard.

3.   Repeat this process with the oranges.

4.   To assemble, add the grapes to the bowl of citrus segments along with the orange blossom water, then sprinkle over the citrus sugar. Gently toss everything together until the sugar has dissolved. Arrange on a platter and sprinkle over the ground cinnamon.

TIP
Rubbing the citrus zest into the sugar will release the essential oils, ensuring better flavour. This is a good tip when baking cakes, too – see the Grapefruit Drizzle Traybake on page 44.

aubergines with whipped feta, grapefruit + hot honey

Serves 2-3

2 small aubergines (eggplants)
    (about 400g/14oz in total),
    cut into quarters lengthways
40ml (1½fl oz/1⅔ tbsp) olive oil
¼ tsp fine sea salt
1 red grapefruit, peeled, segmented
    and segments sliced in half again
small handful of fresh mint leaves,
    to garnish

for the hot honey
1 red chilli, finely sliced
2 tbsp honey
juice of ½ lime
2 tbsp water

for the whipped feta
150g (5oz) feta
100g (3½oz) Greek yoghurt
zest of ½ lemon
1 tbsp extra-virgin olive oil
freshly ground black pepper

equipment
food processor or blender

This dynamic combination brings together salty, sour, bitter, sweet and heat. It works well served with some pitta bread as part of a vegetarian meal, but it would also exist very happily alongside lamb.

Both feta and Greek yoghurt can vary quite a lot in terms of thickness so you might find that the whipped feta comes out thicker or looser than you were expecting – this is not a problem, it will taste good either way!

1. Preheat the oven to 220°C fan/240°C/475°F/gas 9. Line 1-2 baking trays with baking parchment.

2. Spread out the aubergine quarters on the prepared baking trays, brush the cut sides with the olive oil, then lightly sprinkle over the salt (the feta is salty so season the aubergines sparingly). Roast in the oven for 25 minutes until soft and a deep golden brown.

3. To make the hot honey dressing, combine the ingredients in a small pan and bring to a bubble, then reduce the heat to low and cook for about 2–3 minutes. You can add a splash of water to loosen the consistency if needed. Remove from the heat.

4. For the whipped feta, combine the feta, yoghurt and lemon zest in a food processor and blend. While the processor is running, drizzle the olive oil through the funnel until the feta is smooth, light and whipped – if it's too thick, you can add more yoghurt, olive oil or a scant tablespoon of water. Season with pepper.

5. To serve, spread the whipped feta over a serving plate, then arrange the roasted aubergine slices on top, followed by the grapefruit pieces, mint leaves and the sliced chilli from the honey dressing. Drizzle over a spoonful of the honey sparingly as it is quite hot!

salmon tacos with grapefruit + avocado

Serves 4

4 salmon fillets, about 150–200g
    (5–7oz) each, skinned and
    pin-boned

for the spice rub
½ tbsp cumin seeds, toasted and
    ground
1 tsp hot paprika
1 tsp dried oregano
½ tsp cayenne pepper (or chilli flakes)
1 tsp garlic powder
¼ tsp fine sea salt
1 tsp maple syrup
2 tbsp vegetable oil

for the avocado crema
juice of 1 lime, or to taste
¼ tsp fine sea salt
30g (1oz/2 tbsp) creamed coconut
    (or coconut cream)
1 tbsp freshly boiled water (omit if
    using coconut cream)
flesh of 1 avocado
20g (¾oz) fresh coriander (cilantro),
    leaves and stalks
1 green chilli, deseeded
1cm (½in) piece of fresh root ginger,
    peeled and roughly chopped
½ small garlic clove, grated
½ tsp maple syrup

for the grapefruit salsa
1 red grapefruit, peeled, segmented
    and roughly chopped
10 radishes, trimmed and quartered
½ cucumber, thinly sliced into half
    moons
pinch of flaky sea salt

to serve
9–12 tacos (soft or hard, according to
    preference) or tostadas
small handful of mint leaves
small handful of pumpkin seeds, lightly
    toasted

equipment
stick blender or food processor

This is a versatile recipe: equally as perfect for a weeknight dinner as it is for a weekend taco party (simply scale up the quantities). It has a lovely balance of flavours and textures: spice and bitterness from charred salmon and fresh grapefruit, acidity from lime, freshness from cucumber, creaminess from avocado and crunch from radishes.

I am indebted to Milli Taylor for this way of cooking salmon, which ensures a crisp, charred outside and juicy inside.

If you opt for traditional corn tortillas (made with masa harina), this recipe becomes gluten-free.

1. Preheat the oven to 160°C fan/180°C/350°F/gas 4. Line a baking tray with foil.

2. To make the spice rub, toast and grind the cumin seeds, then combine with the paprika, oregano, cayenne and garlic powder, and mix with the salt, maple syrup and oil to form a paste. Lay the salmon fillets on the baking tray and coat with the spice rub (use your hands).

3. Heat a heavy-based frying pan (skillet) over a high heat until very hot, then add the salmon fillets and sear well on all sides (45–60 seconds per side). Return the salmon fillets to the baking tray. (You may have to do this in batches, depending on the size of your tray – you don't want to crowd them as this will prevent you getting a good crust on your salmon.)

4. Transfer the salmon to the oven, cook for 5 minutes, then remove to rest.

5. For the avocado crema, I find it easiest to use a stick blender. Simply combine the ingredients in a tall container (or jug) and blend until thick and creamy. If using a food processor, use the small bowl: combine the lime juice, salt, coconut cream and boiled water and blend until smooth, then add the rest of the ingredients and blend. Add more lime juice or salt, to taste, or an extra splash of water, if needed, to get the right consistency.

6. For the grapefruit salsa, combine the ingredients in a small serving bowl and mix gently.

7. When ready to serve, warm through your tacos, if liked. Then put all the elements in the middle of the table and allow everyone to build their own. To build a taco, I recommend a spoonful of the avocado crema, followed by the salsa, then flakes of salmon. Garnish with mint leaves and a sprinkling of toasted pumpkin seeds.

curried corn fritters with grapefruit dipping sauce

Serves 2-4

1 tsp cumin seeds, toasted
1 tsp coriander seeds, toasted
1½ tsp fenugreek leaves, fresh
    or dried
70g (3oz/⅔ cup) chickpea (gram)
    flour
1 tsp ground turmeric
1 tsp garlic powder
¾ tsp fine sea salt
freshly ground black pepper
90ml (3fl oz/6 tbsp) water
neutral oil (e.g. vegetable), for frying
1 x 200g (7oz) tin corn, drained
15g (½oz) fresh coriander (cilantro),
    finely chopped, plus extra to
    serve
2 spring onions (scallions), thinly sliced
flaky sea salt, to garnish
mint leaves, to serve

for the dipping sauce

4 tbsp fresh grapefruit juice
    (about ½ grapefruit)
1 tbsp rice wine vinegar
1 tsp caster (superfine) sugar
1 red chilli, finely chopped (add the
    seeds if you want it spicier)

TIP

Most batters – whether for Yorkshire puddings, crêpes, blinis, farinata, etc. – benefit from some resting time before cooking, as this allows the flour to properly absorb the liquid. See also the Malted Crêpes (page 112) and Liquorice and Lemon *Zeppole* Doughnuts (page 224).

I fully get the appeal of a tin of corn – so convenient! – but I've also always felt that corn is a bit of a fraud, parading around as a vegetable when it's actually quite sweet. In South and Central America, where corn was originally developed thousands of years ago by those living in modern-day Mexico, corn is often paired with flavours like spicy chilli, sour lime and salty cotija cheese – all of which balance its inherent sweetness. Likewise, in this recipe, the slight bitterness and sourness of the grapefruit in the dipping sauce beautifully balances these fritters, which are more corn than batter (as they should be!).

The batter, however, is not an afterthought: it is headily spiced and made with chickpea flour, a common denominator across India, used in dishes such as pakoras, Gujarati *dhokla* (a savoury fermented cake) and Rajasthani *kadhi* (a yoghurt-based soup).

1. In a pestle and mortar, roughly crush together the cumin and coriander seeds with the fenugreek.

2. Add these to a bowl along with the chickpea flour, turmeric, garlic powder, salt and a few grinds of black pepper, then whisk to ensure everything is evenly dispersed. Gradually add the water, whisking thoroughly until there are no lumps. Add the corn, chopped coriander and spring onions to your batter and stir to coat. Set aside.

3. Make the dipping sauce by mixing the ingredients together in a bowl. I squeeze the grapefruit directly in and am happy when some pulp makes its way into the sauce, both for flavour and appearance. Set aside.

4. Line a plate with kitchen paper. Pour a thin layer of oil into a wide frying pan (skillet) and set over a medium-high heat.

5. When the oil in the frying pan is shimmering, add small spoonfuls of the batter to the pan and use an offset spatula to gently flatten the fritters so that the corn forms a single layer. Avoid overcrowding the pan, otherwise it'll be hard to get the fritters golden brown. Cook for 3–4 minutes until the undersides become lightly browned, then flip and cook for a further 2–3 minutes until evenly golden. Transfer to the paper-lined plate and sprinkle with a little flaky sea salt. Repeat until the batter is used up, adding another thin layer of oil if required.

6. Serve with the dipping sauce and mint leaves alongside.

jerk pork belly with grapefruit hot sauce

Serves 6-8

2kg (4lb 8oz) pork belly, rind scored
2 tbsp flaky sea salt

for the jerk marinade
10 red chillies
2 bunches of spring onions (scallions)
4 garlic cloves, peeled
6cm (2½in) piece of fresh root ginger, peeled
1 tbsp chilli sauce or hot sauce (I like sambal oelek)
100ml (3½fl oz/scant ½ cup) rapeseed (canola) oil
100ml (3½fl oz/scant ½ cup) soy sauce
2 tbsp rice vinegar
1 tbsp allspice berries, toasted and ground
small bunch of thyme
1 tsp flaky sea salt
freshly ground black pepper

for the grapefruit hot sauce
2 red grapefruits: 1 zested (reserved for herb topping), then both peeled
2 red chillies, roughly chopped (deseeded, if preferred)
2 banana shallots, peeled and chopped into 3–4 pieces
50ml (2fl oz/3 tbsp plus 1 tsp) rice vinegar
juice of 1 lime
1 garlic clove, peeled
15g (½oz) fresh root ginger, peeled
4 tbsp soft light brown sugar
pinch of ground cinnamon
1 tsp flaky sea salt

for the herb topping
zest of 1 red grapefruit
30g (1oz) fresh mint, finely chopped
30g (1oz) fresh coriander (cilantro), finely chopped

equipment
food processor or blender

Jamaican jerk can be misunderstood as a specific mix of spices when it is primarily a method of cooking where meat (typically pork or chicken) is seasoned, marinated, then cooked over smouldering pimento wood branches. This is not something we can easily replicate at home, but it's possible to take inspiration, as I have done here: charring the spring onions and chillies that go into the marinade helps to offer a hint of the smokiness that you get with true jerk. This recipe is a crowd-pleaser, delivering soft, moist pork belly, perfect crackling and great flavour (fair warning though: the sauce is hot). If possible, it is best to start marinating the pork belly the night before.

And the hot sauce? My inspiration for this came from the popular grapefruit-flavoured soft drink available across the Caribbean: Ting. You can make this on the same day that you roast the pork belly, but it becomes even more delicious over time, so there's the option to make it several days ahead. I love this served inside a roti along with coleslaw, but you could just as easily knock up some rice and (gungo) peas.

1. Boil the kettle. Place the pork belly on a rack over the sink, then pour the freshly boiled water over the rind. Thoroughly pat dry with kitchen paper, then sprinkle the rind generously with flaky sea salt. Set aside.

2. Set a large frying pan (skillet) over a high heat. When hot, add the chillies, turning them until they are blackened on all sides. Remove and repeat with the spring onions. Don't be timid – you want to take these quite far. Set aside until you're ready to make the marinade.

3. Make the hot sauce. Put the ingredients into a blender and whizz until smooth. Pour this mixture into a saucepan and set over a medium-high heat. Bring to the boil, then reduce the heat and simmer for 12–15 minutes, stirring frequently until the sauce has reduced by a third. Taste and adjust the seasoning if required, then pass through a sieve (fine mesh strainer). Add a spoonful of the mixture left in the sieve back to the strained sauce and discard the rest. Leave the sauce to cool fully, then transfer to a clean (ideally sterilised) jar and place in the fridge (see also Make Ahead note).

4. In the same blender that you used for the sauce (if making on the same day), whizz together all the ingredients for the jerk marinade. Add half the marinade to a shallow ovenproof dish that will fit the pork snugly and place the pork belly on top, flesh-side down. Use your fingers or a spoon to cover the sides of the pork belly with the marinade, being careful not to touch the rind, as this needs to stay very dry to ensure good crackling. Cover with foil and marinate in the fridge overnight. Store the rest of the marinade in a container in the fridge.

5. The next day, preheat the oven to 130°C fan/150°C/300°F/gas 2 and line a shallow roasting tin with foil. Transfer the pork to the roasting tin and cook, uncovered, for 3½ hours.

6. In the last 30 minutes of cooking, prepare the herb topping by combining the ingredients in a small dish. Separately, put the remaining jerk marinade into a small pan and bring to a simmer over a medium heat. Remove from the heat and set aside.

7. Remove the pork belly from the oven and increase the heat to 220°C fan/240°C/475°F/gas 9. Carefully slice the crackling from the flesh in one piece and place this on a separate foil-lined baking tray. Return the crackling to the oven and roast for a further 15–20 minutes, or until perfectly golden. Break the crackling into shards.

8. Serve the pork belly sliced, with the herb topping scattered across the top and crumbled shards of crackling. Serve the warmed jerk marinade and hot sauce alongside.

MAKE AHEAD

The hot sauce can be made a week or two in advance and stored in the fridge. The jerk marinade can be made up to 3 days in advance and stored in the fridge.

TIP

A general rule of thumb is to make sauces that involve spices and stronger flavours in advance, as this gives the flavours time to develop and harmonise. This is true of the marinade and hot sauce in this recipe, but also dishes like curries, which taste better the day after they're made.

duck confit with bitter orange salsa verde

Serves 3–4

4 duck legs, skin on

¾ tbsp flaky sea salt

1 tbsp coriander seeds, toasted and lightly crushed

500g (1lb 2oz) unsalted butter, cut into large slices

for the salsa verde

2 x 5mm (¼in) slices of Seville orange (or red grapefruit), pips removed

150ml (5fl oz/scant ⅔ cup) extra-virgin olive oil, plus ½ tbsp for the orange

10g (¼oz) fresh oregano

10g (¼oz) fresh mint

½ garlic clove, grated

¼ tsp fine sea salt

equipment

stick blender (or food processor)

SUSTAINABLE TIP

The leftover fat can be reused for future duck confit! Every time you use it, there will be more and more duck flavour, making this a delicious, sustainable and more cost-effective recipe to reproduce each time. Strain the impurities from the duck fat using a fine sieve or muslin and keep it in a sterilised jar or airtight container in the fridge – it will last indefinitely (no, really).

MAKE AHEAD

Store the cooked duck in the fat for up to 5 days before gently reheating to melt the fat. Proceed with step 4.

Duck confit will always recall classic bistros in Paris for me. I imagined that making it would be complex and technical, best left to the professionals, but it's ludicrously straightforward – just three core ingredients and pretty hands-off, not to mention delicious!

This is ideal for a relaxed dinner party: the oven does the majority of the work for you, while the sauce is the work of mere moments (and a blender). Duck and orange are a tried-and-tested combination, but here Seville orange brings forth its bitterness in a salsa verde recipe adapted from Nancy Silverton, offering an antidote to the melting duck flesh and rich crispy skin. Serve with mashed potatoes.

1. Preheat the oven to 150°C fan/170°C/325°F/gas 3.

2. Place the duck legs in a cast-iron casserole (Dutch oven) or ovenproof dish that fits them snugly in a single(ish) layer. Sprinkle with the salt and coriander seeds, then cover with the butter. Wrap the dish tightly with a couple of sheets of kitchen foil and bake for 2½ hours.

3. Remove from the oven, allow to cool for 5–10 minutes, then transfer the duck legs to a plate. Leave the fat in the dish to cool for a further 5–10 minutes, then strain through a sieve (fine mesh strainer) and transfer to an airtight storage container. This can be stored in the fridge indefinitely.

4. To finish the duck, turn the oven up to 220°C fan/240°C/475°F/gas 9, open the windows and boil the kettle. Place the confit duck legs, skin-side up, on a rack set over a roasting tin. Pour 2cm (¾in) boiling water into the roasting tin and place in the oven for 20–25 minutes until the skin is crispy and a dark golden brown all over.

5. Meanwhile, start the salsa verde. On a baking sheet, brush the orange slices with the half tablespoon of olive oil. Bake in the oven for 18–20 minutes (at the same time as the duck, on the shelf above) until starting to char. Transfer to a chopping board and leave to cool for 5 minutes, then chop finely.

6. To make the salsa verde, add the herbs, garlic and salt to a blender, and pulse until finely chopped, then drizzle in the olive oil and process until a smooth sauce forms. Finally, stir in half of the chopped orange and taste – if you're happy to go more bitter, then add the rest.

7. Serve the duck alongside mashed potato with a drizzle of salsa verde and place the rest in a jug on the table.

grapefruit drizzle traybake

Makes 12–16 squares

170g (6oz/¾ cup) caster (superfine)
    sugar
zest of 2 red grapefruits
225g (8oz) unsalted butter
4 eggs
50g (2oz/½ cup) ground almonds
1½ tsp flaky sea salt (yes, 1½ tsp –
    don't panic)
225g (8oz/1¾ cups) self-raising flour
1 tsp baking powder
4 tbsp whole milk (or non-dairy milk)

for the glaze
175g (6oz/¾ cup) granulated sugar
juice of 1 red grapefruit

equipment
electric hand whisk or stand mixer
30 x 25 x 4cm (12 x 10 x 1½in) baking
    tin

TIP
Which cake mixing method?
I use the all-in-one method
for more rustic cakes (such
as this one), where lightness
and evenness of texture are
less important, whereas if I'm
making a more refined, multi-
layered cake I am more likely
to use the creaming method.
Regardless of the method used,
as soon as flour is added be
sure to not overwork the mixture,
otherwise your cake will end up
with a tougher crumb.

I grew up making (and eating) Mary Berry's lemon drizzle traybake. It was the recipe my family always turned to for school bake sales, birthday parties or moments of greed. The genius of Mary's recipe doesn't lie in the cake itself, but in the glaze. So many lemon drizzle recipes get you to spoon a syrup over the cake, and then possibly add an icing over that, but Mary's recipe just requires you to combine lemon juice with granulated sugar – once poured over the cake, the fresh citrus juice soaks right through while the sugar, if given a little time, crystallises on top to create a crunchy glaze. It's perfection.

Grapefruit has a complex sour-sweet-bitter-floral thing going on that is distinctive when eaten raw but tends to get lost when cooked. I suspect this is why grapefruit cakes are not really a thing. Still, I was determined to give grapefruit its time to shine and the reason it works so well here is because of – you guessed it – that glaze. Since the glaze isn't heated, the grapefruit juice retains all the qualities that make it wonderful and simply seeps into the cake. It's my new favourite.

I like this cake best on day 2, but – really – good luck with that.

1. Preheat the oven to 160°C fan/180°C/350°F/gas 4 and line the baking tin with a piece of baking paper (this can be done by roughly pushing a sheet into the tin – this is a rustic cake!).

2. In a large bowl, rub together the caster sugar and grapefruit zest. Add the butter, eggs and ground almonds, sprinkle the salt over evenly, then sift over the flour with the baking powder (to help disperse it evenly). Mix everything together using an electric hand whisk just until fully combined and smooth (don't spend too long on this, as overworking the mixture will result in a tough cake). Briefly whisk in the milk, then pour the batter into the prepared tin and even out the top.

3. Bake for 30–40 minutes until golden and an inserted skewer comes out clean. Leave to cool completely in the tin.

4. To glaze the cake, combine the granulated sugar and grapefruit juice in a jug, then pour the mixture over the cake so that it is evenly covered. Leave to set (around 2–3 hours) before eating.

grapefruit marmalade

Makes 3-4 jars

4 red grapefruits (about 2kg/4lb 8oz)
generous pinch of fine sea salt
1.4 litres (2⅖ pints/5 cups) filtered
    water
700g (1lb 9oz/generous 3 cups)
    granulated (or caster/superfine)
    sugar (see Tip)
juice of 1 lemon

equipment

large non-reactive stock pot or
    jam pan
4–5 sterilised jam jars (I always
    prepare extra, just in case)
sugar thermometer (optional)

TIP

Caster (superfine) and
granulated sugar are not
always interchangeable in
recipes because they can
affect the texture of a cake,
but for recipes like jams and
marmalades either can be
used and it's much more cost-
effective to use granulated.

I love a classic Seville marmalade as much as the next person, but once you have tried this grapefruit one, you might not go back. This has got incredible flavour, beautiful colour and a perfect texture. I cannot take complete credit as it is adapted from a David Lebovitz recipe. Not only is it stunningly delicious, but it has plenty of uses within this book: in the Marmalade Steamed Pudding (page 48), Flourless Coconut and Marmalade Cake (opposite) and the Cocoa Nib Tart, Three Ways (page 202). Try it!

1. Rinse and brush the grapefruits under cold water. Cut each grapefruit in half widthways, then use a spoon to scrape the pulp out of 4 of the grapefruit halves. Coarsely dice the grapefruit pulp and scrape it, along with any juice on the cutting board, into a bowl. Discard the grapefruit skins.

2. Cut the remaining 4 grapefruit halves in half again (to get quarters) and use a sharp knife to cut these crossways into thin slices, about 2.5mm (⅛in) thick. Place the grapefruit slices in the pan along with the salt and enough water to cover. Bring to the boil, then reduce to a simmer and cook for 5 minutes. Turn the heat off and let the grapefruit pieces sit in the hot water until cool.

3. Drain the grapefruit pieces and place them back in the pan along with the chopped grapefruit pulp, measured water, sugar and lemon juice. Bring the mixture to the boil, then pour into a bowl. Cover with a piece of baking paper and refrigerate overnight.

4. The next day, pour the mixture back into a non-reactive pan and bring to the boil, stirring gently and skimming once or twice. Cook until the marmalade gets to 103°C (217°F) on a sugar thermometer (this takes longer than you would expect). When the right temperature is reached, pour the marmalade into a heat-proof jug and allow to cool for 5 minutes.

5. If you don't have a thermometer, you can check the set of your marmalade by putting a few drops of it onto a cold plate. Leave it for a minute or so before checking the consistency: when you drag your finger through it, it should hold (rather than spread out like a syrup). Other visual cues include there no longer being any foam on the surface and the bubbles disappearing.

6. Pour the marmalade into sterilised jars and seal.

flourless coconut + marmalade cake

Serves 8–12

I love coconut, but recognise that it can be quite a sweet and cloying flavour. Here, in this cake adapted from a Belinda Jeffery recipe (via Ottolenghi), the bitterness of marmalade in the cake batter tempers the coconut without overwhelming it. The coconut also serves up texture; cakes made purely with ground almonds can get quite soft, whereas the desiccated coconut in this one adds a slightly more toothsome quality. Incidentally, the whole thing is gluten-free.

1. Preheat the oven to 160°C fan/180°C/350°F/gas 4. Grease the base and sides of the cake tin and place a circle of baking paper in the base.

2. Cream together the butter, sugar, vanilla and orange zest until pale and fluffy, about 3–4 minutes. Whisk in the marmalade and the salt, followed by the eggs, one at a time, until thoroughly incorporated. Fold through the ground almonds and desiccated coconut until fully combined. Transfer the cake batter to the prepared tin and even out the top.

3. Bake for 40 minutes until golden, then allow to cool for around 10 minutes before turning it out of the tin.

150g (5oz) butter, softened, plus extra for buttering the cake tin
130g (4½oz/scant ⅔ cup) caster (superfine) sugar
½ tsp vanilla bean paste
zest of ½ orange
3 tbsp Grapefruit Marmalade (see opposite) (or store-bought marmalade)
¼ tsp fine sea salt
3 eggs
120g (4½oz/1¼ cups) ground almonds
50g (2oz/½ cup) desiccated (unsweetened shredded) coconut

equipment
20cm (8in) sandwich cake tin

marmalade steamed pudding

Serves 6-8

butter, for greasing
150g (5oz) Grapefruit Marmalade
    (page 46) (or store-bought
    marmalade), plus 3 tbsp
125g (4½oz/generous 1 cup)
    shredded vegetable suet
125g (4½oz/generous ½ cup)
    self-raising flour
125g (4½oz/generous ½ cup) caster
    (superfine) sugar
1 tsp baking powder
¼ tsp fine sea salt
2 eggs
50ml (2fl oz/3 tbsp plus 1 tsp) whole
    milk
30ml (1fl oz/2 tbsp) double (heavy)
    cream
zest of ½ orange
½ tsp vanilla bean paste

equipment

1-litre (1-quart) pudding basin
    or Pyrex bowl
stick blender (or small blender)

TIP

I know that suet isn't particularly fashionable these days but, truly, I have found it to be the best option when making steamed puddings – you don't get the right texture with butter.

Britain left its political might in the era of colonialism (thankfully!), but we will forever remain leaders in the category of puddings. I have a deep appreciation for the elegance of desserts: a wobbly, melt-in-the-mouth panna cotta, a towering soufflé, a crispy but marshmallow-y pavlova . . . but nothing beats a Great British pud. The rules are minimal: a British pudding – whether a crumble, a bread and butter pud or a sticky toffee pud – must be served warm, with cream or custard alongside. Beyond this, no perfection or precision is required – just sweet, sweet comfort. Let's face it, we Brits have never been all that good at elegance, but boy do we nail cosy. Which brings me to this steamed sponge. I have always found the classic golden syrup version to be too sweet, but marmalade – with its bitter complexity – makes the perfect substitute.

1. Generously butter your pudding basin and place a circle of greaseproof paper in the bottom. Add the 3 tablespoons of marmalade.

2. In a medium bowl, combine all the dry ingredients: suet, flour, sugar, baking powder and salt.

3. Separately, blend the 150g marmalade until a paste/purée is formed (I find a stick blender easiest for this), then whisk together with the eggs, milk, cream, orange zest and vanilla.

4. Add the wet ingredients to the dry and whisk together until smooth, then pour into the pudding basin, leaving an inch clear under the rim. Cover the surface of the batter with a circle of greaseproof paper, then cover with a double layer of foil. Secure the foil to the basin with a rubber band or string, then trim any excess foil.

5. Place an upturned saucer (I wrap this in foil) in the bottom of a large pan with a lid, then place the pudding on top. Carefully pour water into the pan until it reaches half to two-thirds of the way up the side of the pudding basin. Cover with the lid, gradually bring to the boil, then reduce the heat to low and steam for 2 hours. Top the pan up with boiled water from the kettle halfway through, if needed.

6. Once the pudding is cooked, turn the heat off and remove the pan lid to let the steam escape. Carefully lift the pudding out of the pan and remove the foil and greaseproof paper. Run a small knife around the inside of the basin, place a serving plate on top and turn the pudding out. Serve immediately with cold pouring cream (my personal favourite) or custard. You can serve extra marmalade, loosened with some fresh orange juice or a splash of hot water, if liked.

individual negroni pavlovas

Serves 6-8

for the meringues
(or use store-bought)
5 fresh egg whites (about 130g/4½oz)
240g (8½oz/scant 2½ cups) icing
   (confectioners') sugar
1 tsp lemon juice (or a mild vinegar,
   such as apple cider vinegar)
zest of ½ grapefruit

for the caramel
100g (3½oz/½ cup) sugar
100ml (3½fl oz/scant ½ cup) water
1 star anise
½ tsp coriander seeds, toasted and
   lightly crushed
150ml (5fl oz/scant ⅔ cup) fresh
   grapefruit juice
25ml (1fl oz/1 tbsp plus 2 tsp) fresh
   lemon juice
50ml (2fl oz/3 tbsp plus 1 tsp) Campari

for the gin-spiked cream
2 tbsp icing (confectioners') sugar
pinch of fine sea salt
600ml (1 pint/2½ cups) double
   (heavy) cream
100ml (3½fl oz/scant ½ cup) sour
   cream
4 tbsp gin (I like a London Dry Gin,
   e.g. Tanqueray)

for the topping
3 grapefruits, peeled, segmented
   and drained (see page 30)
3 amaretti biscuits (optional)

equipment
electric hand whisk or stand mixer

This dessert is an evolution of one I cooked on *MasterChef* (but this time designed to be less of a faff and easier to get right!). The elements and flavours of the original dessert have been reborn here as a pavlova, which is always a crowd-pleaser. Truthfully, I've never been a fan of meringue – I find it a blandly sweet concoction; it needs the oomph of something sour or bitter to counteract the sweetness. Grapefruit bolstered with Campari (see also the Grapefruit Margarita cocktail on page 55) and a gin-spiked cream places the flavour profile in the realm of a Negroni – that intensely bitter cocktail that people either love or hate (appropriate, really, as the original dessert was a tribute to my dear late friend, Robert, who was famous for his delicious but lethal sloe gin Negronis). It is a perfect example of bitter on bitter (grapefruit, Campari, gin), soothed with cream and (slightly) offset by sweetness.

The meringues can be baked the night before and left in the oven overnight. Please know that meringue is a temperamental beast affected by all sorts of conditions outside of your control, such as temperature and humidity, so if it doesn't turn out perfectly, do not take it personally (as I have done, far too many times).

1. Preheat the oven to 120°C fan/140°C/275°F/gas 1 and line a baking tray with greaseproof paper or a silicone baking mat.

2. To make the meringue, place the egg whites in a scrupulously clean bowl and whisk until soft peaks are achieved. Gradually add the sugar, a spoonful at a time, whisking well to incorporate between each addition. You should end up with a stiff, glossy, white meringue. Add the lemon juice and whisk again, adding another spoonful of sugar if you feel that the mixture has softened a little too much. At the very last minute, fold the grapefruit zest through the meringue and then create 6–8 individual meringue nests on the prepared baking tray. I find it easiest to scoop out the meringue using an ice cream scoop, then use the back of a spoon to spread out the meringue a little and create little craters in the middle.

3. Bake the meringues for 40 minutes, turning the oven down to 100°C fan/120°C/250°F/gas ½ after the first 10 minutes. Once cooked, turn off the oven and leave the meringues to cool in there for at least 2½ hours, or overnight.

4. For the grapefruit and Campari caramel, put the sugar, water, star anise and coriander seeds in a heavy-based pan and set over a medium heat. Cook gently, tipping the pan every so often, until the sugar has dissolved. Turn the heat up so that the sugar starts to caramelise. Do not step away from the pan. Take the sugar to a stage where it is a deep golden brown, then stir in the citrus juices and Campari. The caramel will seize when you do this, but do not panic, just allow the heat to melt the caramel back down. When it's smooth and glossy again, boil it for another 30 seconds, then remove from the heat, strain out the spices and leave to cool completely.

5. Just ahead of assembling the pavlovas, make the gin-spiked cream. In a large bowl, add the icing sugar and a pinch of salt to the double cream and whip until thickened but not quite holding. Gently fold in the sour cream, followed by the gin.

6. Slice half of the grapefruit segments for the topping into smaller pieces.

7. An hour before you want to serve, partially assemble the pavlovas. Add a spoonful of the caramel along with some of the chopped grapefruit into the base of each pavlova. Add a generous dollop of the gin cream on top, flatten out slightly with the back of a spoon, then set aside. Just before serving, drizzle over more grapefruit caramel, top with 2–3 grapefruit segments, then crumble the amaretti biscuits over the top (if using). Serve only to Negroni fans.

MAKE AHEAD

The meringues can be made up to 1 day ahead and should be stored in an airtight container at room temperature or in the oven. Refresh them in a low oven if they've softened a bit. The caramel can also be made ahead and stored in the fridge for 2–3 days – just bring to room temperature before using.

TIP

I like to whip cream by hand (rather than with an electric hand whisk), because it gives me greater control. You also want to err on the side of under-whipping the cream, as when you start agitating it with a spoon it will thicken up further.

pomegranate + campari granita

Serves 4 (or 8–10 as a palate cleanser)

450ml (15fl oz/1¾ cups) pomegranate
juice (I use the POM brand)
1 tbsp caster (superfine) sugar
3 tbsp Campari
1½ tbsp fresh lemon juice

For a long time the concept of granitas was lost on me. Flecks of flavoured ice? No cream, no chocolate, no salted caramel, no butter? Hard pass – and hand me a sticky toffee pudding, please. But then, in Rome, I tried espresso granita with vanilla-spiked whipped cream and I simply couldn't get over how something *that* simple could be *that* good. How could flavoured ice be so . . . *flavourful*? I've been hooked ever since.

Granitas give you much the same satisfaction as a sorbet but I reckon they're even better. For one, they require little of their maker: some juicing or blending, a couple of stirs, a few scrapes with a fork. No ice cream maker required. But also, it is their very lack of requirements – unlike sorbets, you don't need a certain percentage of sugar to achieve a smooth texture – that means they can pack a real flavour punch. I am also obsessed with the shaved ice texture: so satisfying.

Whenever I serve a granita at a private dinner or event, guests always go mad for it; it's the sleeper hit, time and time again. In sum: granitas are both elegant and bold – two things I aspire to be, always. And this granita is the boldest. It's a grown-up, intense vibe that almost leaves you a bit light-headed. It's divine and needs no embellishment in my opinion. This is best served in chilled glasses as soon as it's ready.

Do be sure to use pure pomegranate juice, rather than one that's had water or sugar added.

1. Combine all the ingredients in a jug and stir until the sugar has dissolved. Pour into a shallow freezer-proof container (a metal baking tray is ideal) and place it flat on a shelf in your freezer, uncovered.

2. When 30–45 minutes have elapsed, pass a fork through the mixture – it should have started to freeze at the edges. Return the tray to the freezer and repeat this process 2–3 more times. (Do bear in mind that how quickly the granita freezes will depend mostly on the size and material of the container that you use – you may need to check it more or less frequently than every 45 minutes.)

3. After 3–4 hours you should have a lovely heap of garnet-coloured ice shavings ready to serve.

STORAGE

If you plan to keep the granita over several days, store in a sealed container in the freezer. Remove from the freezer around 5–10 minutes before serving, to ensure it softens enough for you to run a fork through the ice crystals.

grapefruit margarita

Makes 2

Sorry to lure you in under false pretences, but this isn't – strictly speaking – a margarita. It is, in fact, my version of a siesta. A siesta is like a margarita, except the Cointreau becomes Campari and, if you're a fan of bitterness, as I am, then I think you'll like this even better. It's a fresh and flirty cocktail that's great for a party and perfect to whet the appetite ahead of a feast.

A siesta wouldn't typically have a salt rim, but I've included one here because I love the way that it allows the drinker to adjust the flavour profile of their own cocktail. You'll remember from the introduction to this book that salt actually neutralises bitterness, and this is a fun way of playing with that.

1. Prepare your chilled cocktail glasses with salt rims – I like to apply this to half the glass, so that whoever's drinking can choose whether they want salt or not.

2. Add the ingredients to a shaker (or large jar) and fill with ice. Shake until the sides of the shaker are ice-cold, around 30–45 seconds, then strain into the prepared cocktail glasses.

flaky sea salt, for the salt rim
120ml (4fl oz/½ cup) tequila
    (or mezcal, if you're a fan
    of smoky flavours)
40ml (1½fl oz/2 tbsp plus 2 tsp) fresh
    lime juice
1 tbsp agave (or maple syrup)
    or to taste
30ml (1fl oz/2 tbsp) Campari
60ml (2fl oz/4 tbsp) fresh grapefruit
    juice
ice, for shaking

equipment

2 chilled cocktail glasses
cocktail shaker (or large jar)
cocktail strainer or small sieve (fine
    mesh strainer)

TIP

Cocktails provide a great opportunity to better understand your palate (see page 13), as it's quick and simple to taste what you've made and then add a bit more sweetness, or sourness, or bitterness, depending on your preference.

bitter leaves

Most greens and leaves have a degree of bitterness. Lettuces, radicchios, cabbages, kales, chards and herbs all have their nuances: some are milder, some more peppery; some lose substantial volume when you apply heat (looking at you, spinach), while others hold their own. Despite these differences, when cooked many are relatively interchangeable, making the recipes in this chapter conveniently versatile.

Some of the most popular bitter leaves are dark leafy greens: the various types of kale, chard, mature spinach, mustard greens, etc. These add depth, balance and, of course, nutrition to dishes. Bitterness in these vegetables often correlates with their nutrient density and these dark leafy greens truly pack a potent nutritive punch. They are a source of vitamin C (healthy skin, hair and teeth; immune system), vitamin A (healthy skin and vision) and vitamin K (strong bones; proper blood clotting). And where you have dark leafy veg you have chlorophyll, which contains magnesium, a nutrient critical to the proper functioning of the muscular and nervous systems. Popeye wasn't wrong, either: spinach is a brilliant source of protein, iron and beta-carotene (which stimulates collagen production).

Beyond the dark leafy pack, there are brighter, crisper salad leaves (younger spinach, rocket, watercress, endive, milky white bulbs of chicory, lettuce), wine-coloured radicchios in all their varieties, hardy brassicas (Brussels sprouts, cabbages), celery (in its own category, with an undeniable bitter edge) and herbs (often treated as a garnish when they are an ingredient in their own right – don't let the small supermarket packets fool you). All of these bring good things to the table in terms of flavour, texture and health.

Radicchios represent the bitterest and most beautiful of the bitter leaves. They bring much-needed colour to the winter months, in addition to waking up our palates from all the heavy, creamy meals that we tend to eat during this season. Radicchios have much complexity of flavour and – moderated by a little sweetness, creaminess or saltiness – they shine.

Bitter leaves generally love nothing more than cheese and, really, this makes a lot of sense: cheese offers creaminess and saltiness, which soothes and offsets the natural astringency of the leaves. We see this in Italian *gnudi* (ravioli filled with spinach and ricotta), in Cypriot *spanakopita*, in Indian *saag paneer*, in American mac'n'greens and in Persian *sabzi khordan* (a platter of herbs served alongside a meal, often with feta).

The attitude to, and availability of, bitter leaves varies widely worldwide. In Italy, they love intense greens like *cicoria* and *puntarelle*, as well as all variations of radicchio. In Iran, an abundance of herbs can be found in most meals. In the US, you can easily source piquant mustard greens and broccoli rabe. In the UK, however, there is less on offer: it's either spinach, kale, watercress or rocket; radicchios and chicory too, but they are harder to find.

Sadly, bitter leaves are being tamed. Plants that used to be wild, grassy, primitive have been trained, managed and contained to facilitate their production en masse. We're losing precisely what made them healthful in the first place. Where bitter leaves used to be distinctly vegetal, they are now increasingly neutral – think of supermarkets that celebrate a bag of spinach for its mild flavour. Visiting my friend Miss P's allotment is a stark reminder that it wasn't always this way: the pepperiness of the rocket and celery, picked straight out of the soil, practically knocks you out. Bring back the bitterness!

burrata, radicchio + olive oil breadcrumbs

Serves 2

250g (9oz) burrata

for the breadcrumbs

25g (1oz/scant ½ cup) panko
  (or homemade) breadcrumbs
1½ tsp extra-virgin olive oil
½ tsp flaky sea salt

for the radicchio

1½ tsp extra-virgin olive oil, plus extra
  for drizzling
1 radicchio, leaves torn into large
  strips or pieces
1½ tsp balsamic vinegar, plus extra
  for drizzling
freshly ground black pepper

This is simplicity at its best: mild, creamy burrata against bitter radicchio (it's that soothing quality of dairy again!) with the balsamic delivering both acidity and sweetness. The breadcrumbs here are essentially *pangrattato*, the 'poor man's Parmesan' of southern Italy, and this offers up essential texture. All in all a pretty perfect combination, inspired by social media photos of a similar dish produced by Towpath Café in London (which I've yet to try!). Serve with toasted sourdough.

I like the round Italian variety of radicchio called *chioggia* for this dish.

1. Toast the breadcrumbs with the olive oil in a small frying pan (skillet) over a medium heat until golden. Stir through the salt, then transfer the breadcrumbs to a separate plate.

2. Place the same pan back over a medium heat and heat the olive oil for the radicchio. When hot, add the radicchio and toss to coat in the oil. Add salt and cook for 1–2 minutes until wilted. Remove from the heat and add the balsamic vinegar (it should sizzle) and a twist or two of black pepper.

3. To serve, arrange a burrata ball on each plate (I personally like to tear them apart a bit, so that the cream in the middle starts to ooze out), then top with the radicchio followed by a blanket of breadcrumbs. Drizzle over a little extra olive oil and, if you'd like a bit of extra sweetness to counteract the bitterness of the radicchio, a touch of balsamic as well. Best eaten immediately (as if you needed any encouragement).

tabbouleh fritters

Makes around 14

150g (5oz/scant 1 cup) bulgur wheat, soaked in cold water for 1–2 hours, then drained

100g (3½oz) flat-leaf parsley, finely chopped (stalks and all)

150g (5oz) feta cheese, crumbled unevenly

¼ tsp chilli flakes, or to taste (*pul biber* is particularly nice here)

1 egg

½ garlic clove, grated

1 tbsp plain (all-purpose) flour

pinch of baking powder

zest of ½ lemon

1 tsp flaky sea salt

freshly ground black pepper

3–4 tbsp olive oil, for frying

equipment

food processor

TIP

A hot pan and plenty of fat is key to crispy fritters. Also: resist the temptation to move them around. (See also the Curried Corn Fritters on page 36.)

I cannot begin to describe how moreish these are: toothsome from the bulgur wheat, salty from the feta and fresh from all that parsley, whose innate bitterness brings the fritters into balance. They are, of course, inspired by that classic Middle Eastern salad *tabbouleh* and – just as in that dish – the parsley is not merely a herb offered up for a bit of additional flavour, it is used as a green leafy vegetable in its own right. These make a perfect snack served with the Tahini Yoghurt Sauce from page 90, or you can turn them into a light lunch by serving them alongside a tomato salad dressed with pomegranate molasses.

When it comes to the bulgur wheat, I like to use the cold soaking method, which requires a bit of forethought (either the night before, or a couple of hours ahead of when you want to cook the fritters) but zero effort.

1. In a food processor, process half of the soaked bulgur wheat with the parsley and two thirds of the feta. Tip the mixture into a large bowl, then add the rest of the ingredients (except the oil). Mix everything with your hands for a couple of minutes until it's easier to work with and starts to hold together. Test the seasoning and adjust accordingly. Chill the mixture in the fridge for an hour or so.

2. When the mixture has firmed up, form it into small, slightly flattened patties, about 4cm (1½in) in diameter.

3. Heat the oil in a non-stick frying pan (skillet) over a high heat and line a baking tray with a double layer of kitchen paper. When the pan is hot, pan-fry a few fritters at a time, being careful not to overcrowd the pan. They're delicate, so resist the temptation to touch them while they're cooking – you want them to develop a golden crust and this will not happen if you interfere. They should take a good 5–7 minutes (maybe even more) each side. Remove from the pan to drain on the kitchen paper and eat immediately (or keep warm in a low oven).

raw kale + grapefruit salad

Serves 2

100g (3½oz) cavolo nero (black kale)
2 spring onions (scallions)
1 tsp fresh dill
30g (1oz/⅓ cup) flaked (slivered)
    almonds
½ grapefruit
40g (1½oz) ricotta salata
    (or Parmesan)
freshly ground black pepper

for the dressing
½ banana shallot (or 1 normal
    shallot), very finely diced
30ml (1¼fl oz/2 tbsp) white balsamic
    vinegar
¼ tsp fine sea salt
60ml (2½fl oz/4 tbsp) extra-virgin
    olive oil

The best kale salad is a pampered one: massaging the kale with the dressing makes a huge difference to the texture and is an essential step. This serves two, but it's so good I could eat it all single-handedly, so it might be worth doubling the recipe. You can also add cooked grains to bulk it out.

1. Start with the dressing: place the shallots in a jar along with the balsamic vinegar and salt, then set aside to soak for 15 minutes. Add the extra-virgin olive oil and shake to combine.

2. Next, prep all your salad ingredients. De-stem the cavolo nero and then shred the leaves widthways into very fine ribbons. Finely slice the spring onions and chop the dill. Toast the flaked almonds, if you like. Peel, segment and finely chop the grapefruit. Finely grate the ricotta salata (or Parmesan).

3. In a large bowl, combine the cavolo nero with the dressing and massage together to soften the leaves. Add the rest of the ingredients (but hold back a tablespoon or so of the cheese) and toss to combine. Sprinkle over the remaining cheese and serve.

TIP
I swear by having a bottle of white balsamic vinegar in your cupboard for seasoning your food. The beauty of it is that it is both sour and sweet, a combination that makes food more moreish. Chefs will often use a *gastrique* (caramelised sugar, deglazed with vinegar) to help enhance the flavour of their sauces: white balsamic is the ready-made equivalent.

bitter greens *börek*

Serves 2-3

for the filling

500g (1lb 2oz) bitter greens
(e.g. Swiss chard, kale,
callaloo, etc.), stems removed
2 garlic cloves, peeled
75g (3oz) mixed fresh herbs (I like
parsley and dill)
4 spring onions (scallions), finely sliced
2 tsp grated nutmeg
¾ tsp maple syrup
45g (1¾oz/⅓ cup) plain (all-purpose)
flour
2 eggs
zest of ½ lemon
½ tsp fine sea salt
freshly ground black pepper
120g (4½oz) feta cheese, crumbled

to assemble

8 sheets yufka or filo (phyllo) pastry
100ml (3½fl oz/scant ½ cup) olive oil
(or melted butter)
1 egg, beaten
sesame seeds, for sprinkling

equipment

food processor

For a while we were all obsessed with the Greek and Cypriot dish *spanakopita* and now it's *börek* – another filo-pastry-based pie, this time in spiral form, which can be found across the Anatolian, Balkan and Middle Eastern regions. My first experience of *börek* was Spasia Dinkovski's drool-worthy pies, which took off during lockdown. There is clearly a long tradition of making *börek* and a lot of skill that goes into it. This dish is merely inspired by that craft, and the charm is that it's both fun to make and fun to eat. It's also delicious served with the Tahini 'Mayo' from page 86.

1. Preheat the oven to 180°C fan/200°C/400°F/gas 6.

2. Bring a large pan of salted water to the boil, add the greens and garlic and simmer for 5 minutes. Drain well, patting the leaves dry with kitchen paper.

3. Place the greens and garlic in a food processor along with all the other filling ingredients (except the feta). Pulse until well blended, then fold in the feta by hand.

4. To assemble, take a sheet of pastry, place on a clean work surface and brush with some of the olive oil. Lay another sheet of pastry on top. Brush some olive oil over a third of this pastry sheet and place a fresh sheet of pastry on top of this area, so that it's offset from the original couple of sheets (the idea is to make one long strip of pastry). Brush the sheet with olive oil and place another sheet on top, then repeat the off-setting technique. In the end you will have four pieces of double-layered pastry, overlapping in a line.

5. The best way to describe the next part of the process is to imagine that you're making sausage rolls. Along one long edge of your pastry, begin to lay out the filling in a line, continuing right to the other end of the pastry, then carefully start to roll the pastry around the filling until you have one long cylinder of pastry filled with the greens and feta mixture. Curl this around on itself like a snail's shell until you have a spiral shape shape (it may split slightly in parts, that's okay!), then place on a baking tray lined with baking parchment.

6. Brush the *börek* with the beaten egg and bake for 40–45 minutes, or until golden brown. Garnish with sesame seeds and allow to cool slightly before eating.

chicory gratin

Serves 3-4

2 tbsp butter
4-5 chicory (around 500g/1lb 2oz),
    cut in half lengthways
¼ tsp fine sea salt
125ml (4fl oz/½ cup) light beer
    or lager

for the sauce

50g (2oz) butter
50g (2oz/scant ½ cup) plain
    (all-purpose) flour
400ml (13fl oz/generous 1½ cups)
    whole milk
2 tsp Dijon mustard
½ tsp fine sea salt
¼ tsp grated nutmeg
freshly ground black pepper

to assemble

8-10 slices of French ham (optional)
100g (3½oz) Gruyère cheese, grated

equipment

balloon whisk
baking dish that snugly fits the
    chicory halves

TIP

When making a béchamel, or any sauce that involves flour, it is essential to cook the flour out properly, otherwise you'll be able to taste it in the final sauce.

This is a delicious, warming dish that hails from Belgium (and Northern France): bitter chicory are braised, wrapped in salty ham, smothered in a mustard-spiked béchamel sauce and showered in umami-rich grated Gruyère. I am indebted to *MasterChef* winner Eddie Scott for alerting me to the beauty of braising the chicory in beer – something that obviously suits the theme of this book. This dish is delicious as a meal in its own right, served with a green salad, but it also works well as a side to meat.

If you'd rather keep this dish meat-free, you can easily leave out the ham, bearing in mind that the bitterness of the chicory will come through a little stronger.

1. Place a large frying pan (skillet) that has a lid over a high heat and add the butter along with the chicory halves, cut-sides down. Cook for around 5 minutes until the chicory have caramelised underneath, then flip them over, sprinkle with the salt and add the beer (it should foam). Cover the pan, turn the heat down a notch or two and allow the chicory to braise until softened, around 10 minutes.

2. Preheat the oven to 220°C fan/240°C/475°F/gas 9.

3. Meanwhile, make your béchamel. Melt the butter in a medium to large saucepan over a medium heat, then whisk in the flour, cooking it out for a couple of minutes. Gradually add the milk a little at a time, whisking as you go to ensure a smooth sauce. Bring the sauce to a simmer and allow to cook for another 2–3 minutes, then season with the mustard, salt, nutmeg and black pepper.

4. When the chicory have braised, use tongs to remove them to a plate lined with kitchen paper to absorb some of the excess liquid. Whisk the remaining braising liquid into the béchamel sauce.

5. To assemble the gratin, wrap each chicory half in a slice of ham and place in the baking dish alongside each other. Pour the béchamel sauce over the top, ensuring everything is covered, then sprinkle over the grated cheese. Bake for around 10–15 minutes until the top of the gratin is nicely golden. Leave to cool for 5–15 minutes before tucking in.

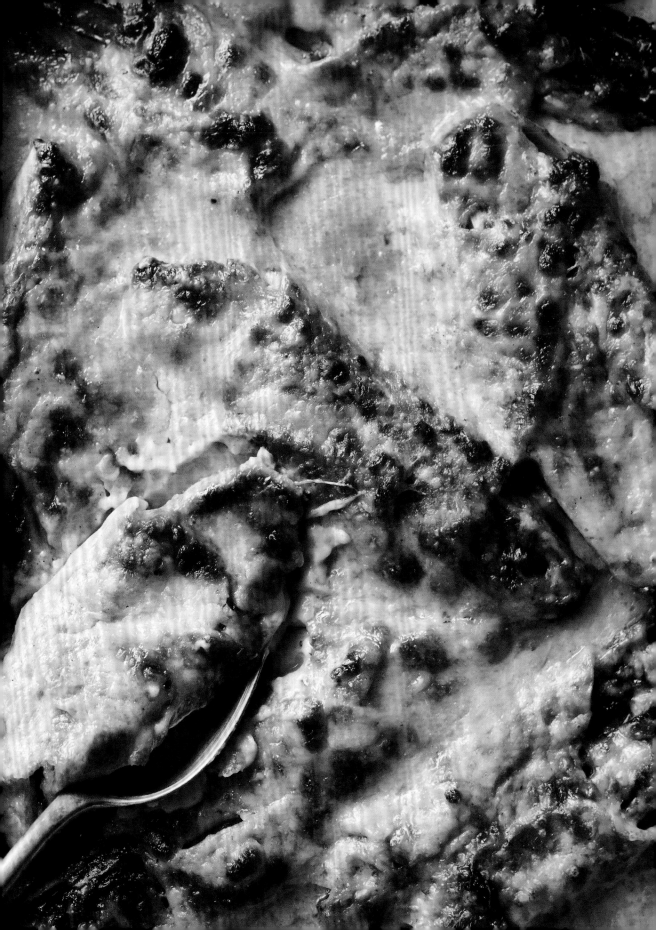

bavette steak with chicory, soy + orange

Serves 2

2 bavette steaks (about 400g/14oz
    total weight)
1 generous tsp Diamond kosher salt
1 tbsp beef dripping or vegetable oil
30g (1oz) butter
2 garlic cloves, lightly bashed with
    the side of a knife
4 fresh thyme sprigs
freshly ground black pepper

for the chicory
juice of 4 oranges (around 200ml/
    7fl oz/scant 1 cup)
2 tbsp tamari (or soy sauce)
2 red (or white) chicory, halved
½ tsp caster (superfine) sugar

A perfect steak needs little embellishment, but I love it served with this sweet-salty-bitter chicory alongside. This is a simple, one-pan dish that delivers on flavour.

Bavette is delicious and cheaper than most other cuts of steak. It's also easier to cook, since it needs to be served quite rare – you're simply looking to develop a really good sear on the outside.

Cooking a good steak is down to a handful of things: the quality of your meat matters, and I also swear by seasoning in advance and basting with butter. If you can, salt your steaks a couple of hours in advance; otherwise, stick to the 15 minutes specified in the recipe.

1. Dry your steaks and season all over with the salt, then set aside for 15 minutes.

2. Separately, combine the orange juice and soy sauce for the chicory and set aside.

3. Get a large heavy-based frying pan (skillet) (cast iron is ideal) and set over a very high heat for 3–4 minutes. If your pan isn't that large, use two – you don't want to overcrowd the pan, otherwise you'll struggle to get a good sear on the steak. Add the beef dripping or vegetable oil, allow to heat up for 30 seconds, then add the steaks. Sear on each side for 1 minute, then again for 30 seconds on each side. Turn the heat down to medium and add the butter, garlic and thyme. As the butter melts and foams, use a spoon to baste the steaks with the butter for 1–2 minutes. Remove the steaks to a plate, pour over the butter, thyme and garlic, season with black pepper, then cover with foil and set aside to rest.

4. Turn the heat back up to high and sprinkle the cut halves of chicory with the sugar. Add the chicory to the pan, cut-sides down, and sear for 1–2 minutes until starting to caramelise. Add the orange juice and soy, turn the heat down to medium and place a lid over the chicory (this can be a lid that fits the pan, or simply a large lid that you can nestle inside the pan to cover the chicory). Braise for around 5 minutes until softened, then remove the lid, turn the heat up and simmer the chicory for a final 1–2 minutes until the glaze has slightly thickened.

5. To serve, flood two plates with the orange and soy glaze, then top each with the sliced steak and two halves of chicory. Serve immediately.

TIP
I use kosher salt to season meat because it's finer than flaky sea salt, so you can achieve a more even coating, and it melts quicker, too.

radicchio, ricotta +
pancetta rigatoni

Serves 2 generously

180g (6oz) dried rigatoni or paccheri
70g (3oz) cubed pancetta
1 red onion, thinly sliced
170g (6oz) radicchio, sliced into
    ribbons about 1.5cm (⅝in) thick
20g (¾oz) Parmesan (or pecorino),
    grated
a few walnuts, toasted (ideally) and
    roughly chopped
freshly ground black pepper
2–3 tbsp fresh ricotta

TIP
This is a good ratio to
remember when cooking
pasta: 1 litre (1 quart)
of water to 1 tablespoon
Diamond kosher salt to
100g (3½oz) pasta.

This bowl of pasta – a dish adapted from the 'Goddess of the Delicious' Nancy Silverton – is a bit different to your usual, but I love it for all of its salty (pancetta), sweet (red onions), bitter (radicchio, walnuts) and creamy (ricotta) flavours.

The difference between quality ricotta and what you buy in the supermarkets (or most food shops, even) is night and day. It's very much not essential here, but if you want a treat, I highly recommend Seirass ricotta.

1. Boil the pasta in a large pan of well-salted water (see Tip) according to the packet instructions (mine takes around 12 minutes to cook, which is enough time to make the sauce). Make sure your walnuts are prepped, as there won't be time for this later.

2. Pan-fry the pancetta in a large dry frying pan (skillet) over a medium-high heat for around 5 minutes: the fat should start to melt and the pieces should start to go golden and crispy.

3. Add the red onion and stir to ensure it is coated in the pork fat. Turn the heat down slightly and pan-fry for 4–5 minutes until the onion has started to soften. Add 1 tablespoon of the pasta cooking water.

4. At this point, your pasta should be ready (but if it's not, just turn the heat under your frying pan down very low to keep things warm while your pasta catches up). Add the radicchio and Parmesan to the frying pan, then use a slotted spoon to scoop the pasta from its water into the pan. Turn the heat up to high and cook for another minute, stirring the pasta. This isn't a saucy pasta, but you can add another tablespoon or so of pasta water if you think it's getting too dry.

5. To serve, divide the pasta between bowls, sprinkle over the chopped walnuts and add a few twists of black pepper. Add a tablespoon or so of ricotta to the side of each bowl and eat immediately.

celery pisco sour

Serves 2

I'm not sure how I got fixated by the idea of a celery cocktail, but it suddenly consumed me. When I tasted this celery pisco sour I knew I had found the perfect vehicle for it – the celery adds a subtle, herbaceous and bitter note that works beautifully with the rich pisco. This is a balanced, refreshing cocktail, perfect for taco night (or, frankly, any night).

The celery syrup will make enough for 7–8 cocktails.

1. Start by making the celery syrup. Combine the ingredients in a saucepan and bring to the boil. Allow to simmer for a couple of minutes, until the sugar is fully dissolved and then take the pan off the heat and allow to cool. If you're intending to store the syrup, then strain out the celery.

2. To make the cocktail, combine all the ingredients except the angostura bitters in a cocktail shaker, top up with ice and shake, then strain straight into the chilled glasses. Garnish with a couple of dashes of the angostura bitters, dragged through with a cocktail stick.

100ml (3½fl oz/scant ½ cup) good-quality pisco
50ml (2fl oz/3 tbsp plus 1 tsp) lime juice
50ml (2fl oz/3 tbsp plus 1 tsp) celery syrup (see below)
2 tbsp egg white
a couple of dashes of angostura bitters, to garnish
ice cubes, for shaking

for the celery syrup
2 celery sticks (about 100g/3½oz), finely sliced
125ml (4fl oz/½ cup) water
250g (9oz/1¼ cups) sugar
⅛ tsp bicarbonate of soda (baking soda)

equipment
cocktail shaker (or large jar)
cocktail strainer or small sieve (fine mesh strainer)
2 chilled cocktail glasses

TIP
The bicarbonate of soda (baking soda) in the celery syrup helps to preserve the fresh green colour.

tahini

When I asked Roy, a Palestinian friend, if he could share some of his feelings about tahini, he replied: 'I don't know what to tell you – tahini is life.' His family come from just outside Nablus, a city renowned for its tahini manufacturers, so this response was probably to be expected. But, given tahini's big flavour, nutritional potency and status in Levantine cuisines, this statement may not be as hyperbolic as it first sounds.

Tahini is documented in Arabic cookbooks as early as the thirteenth century and is a staple in kitchens across the Levant. 'Tahini' comes from the Arabic *tahīniyya*, 'to grind', and it is through the persistent grinding of hulled, dry-roasted sesame seeds that this silky, oily, rich paste is created – a process that has been taking place for thousands of years. The tahini we know is made with white sesame seeds, although black sesame seeds – along with nigella seeds – are used in *qizha*, a black tahini that isn't currently exported outside of the Middle East.

Many of us will be familiar with tahini as an essential ingredient in hummus, where it contributes flavour, richness and texture (supported by the bulk of chickpeas, the heat of garlic and the acidity of lemon). But even though a pot of hummus can now be found in the fridges of many Western households, Roy vividly recalls a time when his British classmates would turn their noses up at the hummus in his lunch box. Still, although the wonders of hummus are evident today, there is certainly room for us to get to know tahini a little better, for it has a life far beyond hummus.

Nutritionally, tahini punches well above its weight: it is full of 'good' fats; a source of fibre; rich in vitamins, minerals, antioxidants and phytonutrients. Regularly eating tahini is linked to lower cholesterol levels, reduced risk of cardiovascular diseases and decreased incidence of cancer. If you're vegan, it is an essential ingredient to have in your cupboard for all the qualities listed above, but also because it is a delicious source of protein that contributes substance to dishes. In short, this simple paste of sesame seeds can support bone, muscle, nerve, heart and mental health: to describe it as nutritionally beneficial is an understatement.

In taste and texture, tahini brings a remarkable and unique set of qualities to the table: smoothness, creaminess, richness, earthiness, nuttiness, smokiness and a subtle, smooth bitterness. Useful in a range of foods (sauces, dips, dressings, soups, marinades), it can be silky, smooth and dense, or pale, light and whipped. It loves lemon, garlic and salt. It is often 'opened' by adding ice water, which initially causes it to seize up before it comes back together into a velvety light sauce. And this points to another of tahini's transformative qualities: it is an emulsifier, holding fat and water molecules together, rather than allowing them to separate. Think of what typically happens when you put a jar of homemade vinaigrette in the fridge: the oil and vinegar separate back into layers. A tahini dressing will not do this: in so many ways, tahini holds things together.

Not all tahini is made equal. The quality of the roasting and grinding processes will affect the flavour, but just as critical is the soil the seeds are grown in, and the minerals it contains. So, when it comes to tahini, it's not about buying local or making it yourself, it's about buying the best. I find these to be the Middle Eastern varieties, as opposed to Greek or Cypriot versions, because they tend to have a more nuanced flavour and silkier texture. (The best sesame seeds in the world are said to be the *humera* variety from Ethiopia – and these are the seeds used by many of the Middle Eastern brands.) Tahini is helpfully shelf-stable after opening, so it can be kept in a cool, dry place for several months (but do smell it before using, to check that the oil has not gone rancid, and give it a brief stir).

Tahini is not dissimilar to peanut butter, and both work in savoury and sweet contexts – indeed, in the Middle East tahini is known as much for being an ingredient in sweet *halva* as in savoury hummus. But in my view, the complexity and bitter edge of tahini reaches beyond PB (which is why tahini on toast ought to make it into your breakfast rotation, see page 82). This chapter embraces the sweet and savoury possibilities of tahini, with dishes (several of which are vegan) that make the most of the richness and body that tahini brings, as well as an indulgent no-churn ice cream (page 94).

For such a tiny seed, sesame truly works wonders and it feels like no coincidence that the expression 'open sesame' – which originated in the Middle Eastern collection of folk tales *One Thousand and One Nights* – has come to refer to the unlocking of treasures. Populations across the Levant have known for many centuries that tahini is exceptionally special – now it's time for the rest of the world to fully catch up.

burnt aubergine dip (*moutabel*)

Serves 2 (or, if you're me, 1)

4 medium–large aubergines (eggplants) that feel dense and heavy for their size

3 tbsp extra-virgin olive oil, plus extra for drizzling

2 tbsp tahini, or to taste

juice of ½ lemon, or to taste

¼ tsp flaky sea salt, or to taste

freshly ground black pepper

fresh pomegranate seeds, to garnish (optional)

fresh mint leaves, to garnish (optional)

I'm dangerously obsessed with this. *Moutabel* is often confused with baba ghanoush, but it is just so much better than that (no disrespect to Baba G). *Moutabel* has fewer embellishments – it does away with the onion, the garlic, the tomatoes – and it also has tahini in it (which, naturally, makes everything better). This has such complexity of flavour (richness, smokiness, creaminess, sharpness, nuttiness, freshness) for what is essentially four ingredients – it has even been known to convert those who don't like aubergines. Think of *moutabel* as vegetarian caviar, best scooped up with either flatbreads or red chicory leaves.

If you like, you can cook the aubergines the day before you want to make this. It's not in any way essential, but this is lovely garnished with pomegranate seeds and fresh mint leaves.

1. Preheat the oven to 200°C fan/220°C/425°F/gas 7.

2. Line a baking tray with foil and lay your aubergines on it. Pierce each aubergine in a few places with the tip of a knife (to prevent any in-oven explosions), then use your hands to smear the skin with 1 tablespoon of the olive oil. Roast for 45 minutes until they are starting to collapse and char.

3. Switch to the grill (broil) setting on your oven, turn the temperature up to maximum and place the tray with the aubergines directly under the grill (broiler). Grill for around 20 minutes until the aubergines are really charred. Remove the aubergines from the oven and place in a bowl, then cover with cling film (plastic wrap). Leave to cool for at least 30 minutes (or you can leave them overnight).

4. When the aubergines are cool, slice open the skins and scoop out the flesh into a bowl. Stir in the remaining 2 tablespoons of oil along with the tahini and lemon juice. Season with salt and pepper, then taste and adjust, adding more tahini, lemon juice and/or salt to taste – it should taste smoky and creamy, with real depth of flavour. To serve, drizzle over a little more olive oil and garnish with pomegranate seeds and mint leaves, if using.

ALTERNATIVES

This also works well with courgettes (zucchini), but cooking times may vary.

tahini *tantanmen* ramen with crispy shiitakes

Serves 2

for the broth

500ml (17fl oz/scant 2 cups)
   vegetable stock
3 medium–large dried shiitake
   mushrooms
1 x 5mm (¼in) piece of fresh root
   ginger, skin on
1 x 5–7cm (2–3in) piece of kombu
   seaweed (optional)
250ml (8½fl oz/generous 1 cup) soya
   milk
1 tbsp tamari (or soy sauce),
   or to taste
70g (3oz/⅓ cup) tahini
1½ tsp sesame oil

to assemble

vegetable oil, for frying
½ leek, sliced about 5mm (¼in) thick
   and rinsed
100g (3½oz) mixed mushrooms (I like
   oyster and chestnut/cremini),
   torn into even bite-sized pieces
fine sea salt and freshly ground
   black pepper
200g (7oz) ready-to-eat udon
   noodles (or noodles of choice)
2 soft-boiled eggs, halved (optional)
1 tbsp peanut rayu
2 spring onions (scallions), cut into
   strips

TIP

When cooking mushrooms,
there are three rules:
1. high heat; 2. refrain from
moving them around too
much; 3. only salt them in
the last couple of minutes of
cooking. This helps to ensure
that they properly caramelise.

This recipe is inspired by *tantanmen* ramen – a Japanese take on Sichuan dan dan noodles, with a broth made from soya milk and sesame – but it is by no means authentic. Typically this would have a proper stock as the base and be topped with minced (ground) pork, but I got attached to the idea of a ramen that could be knocked up quickly and that remained vegetarian/vegan. I also wanted to use udon noodles (again, untraditional), because I love their texture: big, fat, slippery, chewy – is there anything more satisfying?

This is a perfect lunch or dinner for two, in part because the mushrooms and leeks benefit from not being overcrowded when you cook them. It is best to use a Middle Eastern brand of tahini for this recipe.

1. For the broth, bring the stock to the boil, add the shiitakes, ginger and kombu (if using) and simmer for 5 minutes, then turn off the heat and leave to steep.

2. Meanwhile, set a large heavy-based frying pan (skillet) over a medium-high heat and allow to get hot – around 5 minutes. Fish the rehydrated shiitake mushrooms from the broth, remove the stems and thinly slice.

3. Coat the pan with oil, increase the heat to high, then add the leek and all the mushrooms (including the rehydrated shiitake). Do not move them around much – they will take around 10 minutes to get golden and crispy in places. Add a pinch of salt and a few grinds of pepper about 5–10 minutes into cooking.

4. Fish out the ginger from the broth and discard, then add the soya milk, tamari, tahini and sesame oil. Bring to a simmer and allow to bubble for 3 minutes, then check the seasoning and add more tamari if desired. Add the udon noodles and take the pan off the heat, allowing them to warm through in the broth.

5. To plate, use tongs to divide the noodles between two bowls, then ladle over the broth. Top each bowl with half of the crispy mushroom and leek mixture, then add two halves of the soft-boiled eggs (if using). Drizzle each bowl with half a tablespoon of the peanut chilli rayu and garnish with the spring onions.

tahini on toast

Serves 1

1 slice of bread (I like sourdough or
  granary for this)
1 tbsp tahini
1 tsp clear honey, or to taste
  (I buy acacia honey as it
  doesn't crystallise)
¼ tsp ground cinnamon, or to taste

Move over peanut butter, there's a new toast in town: a creamy, smoky and sticky combination of tahini and honey on toasted bread. I say new, but this is commonly eaten in Turkey and Iraq. And while I know that it can hardly be called a recipe, you're welcome nonetheless, because it is wonderful (if messy to eat).

1. Toast the bread to your preference and spread with a thin layer of tahini. Drizzle the honey over the top (but don't take it too close to the edge, as it slips and slides and you can end up in a bit of a sticky mess with it – or is that just me?). Lightly dust over the cinnamon.

2. Toast a second slice of bread when you realise how good it is.

asparagus with sesame seed dressing (*goma-ae*)

Serves 2-4

Preparing vegetables with a sesame dressing is common in Japan, although they would typically grind up the sesame seeds from scratch, whereas here I've used tahini as a shortcut. Don't feel that you need to stick with asparagus: boiled green beans, roasted broccoli or raw, salted cucumber would all work beautifully.

The asparagus has been boiled in this recipe, but you could also grill or roast it.

1. To make the dressing, combine the tahini, tamari, mirin and rice vinegar in a jar and shake until emulsified.

2. Bring a large saucepan of well-salted water to the boil. Drop the asparagus into the boiling water and cook for 2–5 minutes depending on their thickness, then remove with a slotted spoon and drain thoroughly.

3. To serve, spread the dressing over a serving platter then arrange the asparagus spears on top. Sprinkle with the black sesame seeds.

1 bunch of asparagus, woody ends snapped off
1 tsp black sesame seeds, to garnish

for the sesame dressing
60g (2½oz/¼ cup) tahini
1½ tbsp tamari (or soy sauce)
1½ tbsp mirin
½ tbsp rice vinegar

MAKE AHEAD
The dressing can be made up to 5 days in advance and stored in the fridge.

TIP
If you care about the spears staying bright green, plunge them into an ice bath straight after cooking, for 1 minute.

if *panzanella* + *fattoush* had a baby

Serves 4-6

1kg (2lb 4oz) large, dense tomatoes
(e.g. beef tomatoes)
2 tsp flaky sea salt
2 tbsp pomegranate molasses
3 tbsp sultanas (golden raisins),
soaked in 1½ tbsp white
balsamic vinegar
1½ tbsp capers, roughly chopped
2 tbsp sherry (or red wine) vinegar
2 tbsp sesame seeds, toasted
2 bunches of basil, leaves picked

for the croutons
250g (9oz) ciabatta, torn into pieces
5 tbsp extra-virgin olive oil
1 tsp flaky sea salt

for the roasted aubergines
2 medium aubergines (eggplants)
(about 500g/1lb 2oz), cut into
2cm (¾in) discs
1 tsp fine sea salt
3 tbsp olive oil

for the tahini dressing
90g (3¼oz/6 tbsp) tahini
juice of 1 lemon
1 small garlic clove, crushed
2 tbsp extra-virgin olive oil
1-3 tbsp ice-cold water

From Catalonia's *escalivada* to Italy's *panzanella*, and Eritrea's *fata* to the Middle Eastern *fattoush*, countries who enjoy a lot of fresh bread have generally found ways of using it up when it inevitably goes stale. This is a Tuscan *panzanella* that has detoured through Sicily (aubergines and sultanas make an appearance) and cropped up in the Levant, smothered in tahini dressing. It's both moreish and Moorish.

For this recipe, it's best to get all of your ingredients prepped in advance of cooking.

1. Preheat the oven to 220°C fan/240°C/475°F/gas 9. Line 2 large baking trays with baking paper.

2. For the croutons, spread the bread over one of the baking trays, drizzle with the olive oil and sprinkle with salt.

3. For the roasted aubergines, lay the aubergine slices on the second baking tray, brush the cut sides with half of the olive oil then sprinkle with half of the salt. Flip the slices over and repeat.

4. Bake the aubergine and croutons at the same time: the aubergines on the top shelf, the croutons on the bottom. Remove the croutons after around 10 minutes – they should be golden, but with a little softness still in the middle. Remove the aubergines after 30 minutes – they should be cooked through and darkly golden. Once cool enough to touch, tear the aubergine slices into halves.

5. While the croutons and aubergines cook, chop the tomatoes into chunky pieces and place in a colander set over a bowl. Toss with the salt and leave to drain for 10–15 minutes. Transfer the tomatoes to a separate bowl (reserve the bowl of tomato liquid) and stir through the pomegranate molasses. Set aside.

6. In a large serving bowl, combine the croutons with the sultanas (along with their vinegar), capers and sherry vinegar. Set aside.

7. Make the tahini dressing directly in the bowl of tomato liquid. Add the tahini, lemon juice and crushed garlic and whisk together until smooth. Whisk in the olive oil, followed by as much cold water as needed to get it to the consistency of double (heavy) cream.

8. Add the tomatoes and torn aubergines to the bowl with the croutons and sultanas. Pour the dressing over and toss thoroughly. Adjust the seasoning to taste and allow to sit for 15 minutes–1 hour. Add the toasted seeds and basil leaves just before serving.

falafel burgers with tahini 'mayo'

Makes 8 burgers

for the quick-pickled cabbage

500ml (17fl oz/scant 2 cups) water
100ml (3½oz/scant ½ cup) Moscatel or cider vinegar
30g (1oz/2 tbsp) caster (superfine) sugar
20g (¾oz/2 tbsp) fine sea salt
½ white cabbage, tough outer leaves removed, very finely shredded on a mandoline (or with a sharp knife)
1 tsp grated fresh root ginger

for the tahini 'mayo'

juice of 1 lemon
90g (3¼oz/6 tbsp) tahini
90ml (3¼ fl oz/6 tbsp) olive oil
45ml (1½fl oz/3 tbsp) water
2 tsp honey (or maple syrup if vegan)
¼ tsp fine sea salt

for the sweet potatoes

2 garlic cloves, crushed
1 tsp fine sea salt
3 tbsp vegetable oil
2 sweet potatoes, washed and cut into 2cm (¾in) cubes
½ tsp sumac

for the burgers

250g (9oz/generous 1 cup) dried chickpeas (garbanzo beans), soaked in water overnight and drained
45g (2oz) fresh coriander (cilantro)
45g (2oz) flat-leaf parsley
½ large white onion, peeled and cut into 4 pieces
1 garlic clove, peeled
1 tsp fine sea salt
1 tsp ground cumin
1 tsp ground coriander
½ tsp ground cinnamon
1 tsp ground turmeric
2 eggs, beaten
olive oil, for greasing

to serve

8 burger brioche buns
sliced radishes

equipment

food processor
mandoline (helpful, but not essential)
½ cup measure (helpful, but not essential)

I first got into the whole falafel thing when living in Paris as a penniless 21-year-old, where it was a quick and cheap meal to be had in a city of delicious but sometimes pricey food. So when Pilpel, a falafel joint, cropped up to serve London's City workers back in 2009, I was delighted. In a sea of sad desk lunches, Pilpel was a bright light in my banking days.

Veggie burgers are typically more involved to make than a simple beef burger, but so often the result is disappointing: either dry and crumbly or brown and mushy. But the concept of a falafel burger – inspired by those desk-bound falafel lunches – felt like it made sense.

Do not skimp on the lightly pickled cabbage topping here – it provides much needed moisture and piquancy. And the sumac in the sweet potatoes brings a lemon-like acidity, which balances their sweetness.

1. Preheat the oven to 200°C fan/220°C/425°F/gas 7. Line 2 large baking trays with greaseproof paper.

2. Start with the pickled white cabbage. Whisk together all the ingredients (except the cabbage and grated ginger) until the sugar and salt have dissolved. Add the shredded cabbage and set aside.

3. To make the tahini 'mayo', combine the ingredients and whisk together until smooth. Adjust to taste with extra lemon juice and salt. Set aside.

4. For the sweet potatoes, stir together the garlic, salt and 2 tablespoons of the oil in a bowl, then add the sweet potatoes and toss to coat. Arrange the sweet potatoes on one of the prepared baking trays in an even layer and roast in the oven for about 30 minutes.

5. Meanwhile, to make the burgers, combine all the ingredients (except the eggs) in a food processor. Pulse until the mixture is very finely chopped and it holds together when pinched between two fingers. Transfer to a large bowl and mix in the beaten eggs.

6. Brush the greaseproof paper on the remaining baking tray with some oil to prevent the burgers from sticking. The quickest and easiest way to form the patties is to use a ½ cup measure: scoop up the mix, flatten the top then turn out onto the baking tray. Repeat until you have 8 patties. If you don't have a measuring cup, roughly divide the mix into 8 and form the patties using your hands. Brush each one with olive oil and season with a bit more salt.

7. Remove the sweet potatoes from the oven and switch the oven to the grill (broil) setting, letting it heat up to high (5–10 minutes). Meanwhile, use the base of a glass to lightly crush the sweet potatoes, drizzle over the remaining tablespoon of oil along with the sumac, then put back in the bottom of your oven as the grill heats up.

8. Grill the patties for 3–5 minutes, or until they are beginning to brown. Use a spatula to flip each one, then brush with more oil and season with more salt. Grill for a further 2–3 minutes until golden brown.

9. Meanwhile, toast your brioche buns and drain the pickled cabbage, mixing through the grated ginger.

10. To serve, coat the bottom burger bun in the tahini 'mayo', top with a patty, add the pickled cabbage and sliced radishes, then drizzle over a bit more tahini sauce (because you can never have enough). The sweet potatoes can be served inside the burger or alongside.

TIP
Once the burgers have been formed, they can easily be stored in the freezer (with a small sheet of greaseproof paper between each one) and cooked from frozen.

MAKE AHEAD
The pickled cabbage and tahini mayo can be made a couple of days ahead.

allspice chicken, chickpea + tahini *fatteh*

Serves 6

for the confit chickpeas

1 x 400g (14oz) tin chickpeas
   (garbanzo beans), drained
5 garlic cloves, sliced very finely
1 red chilli, slit lengthways
1 tsp cumin seeds, roughly crushed in
   a pestle and mortar
1 tsp coriander seeds, roughly
   crushed in a pestle and mortar
1 tsp Kashmiri chilli powder
¼ tsp chilli (hot pepper) flakes
1 tsp caster (superfine) sugar
100ml (3½fl oz/scant ½ cup) olive oil
½ tsp fine sea salt

for the chicken

1 whole chicken (around 1.5kg/3lb)
1½ tsp ground allspice
1 tbsp olive oil
2 tsp fine sea salt
freshly ground black pepper
1 lemon, halved
1½ tsp sumac
1 tbsp pomegranate molasses

for the tahini sauce

250g (9oz) natural yoghurt
100g (3½oz/scant ½ cup) tahini
juice of 1 lemon
4 tbsp water
1 tbsp date molasses (or ½ tbsp
   honey)

for the tomato sauce

500g (1lb 2oz) ripe tomatoes
½ green chilli
1 tsp cumin seeds, toasted and
   ground
4 tbsp extra-virgin olive oil
salt, to taste

for the croutons

3 flatbreads (*khobez*, if you can
   find it)
a good glug of olive oil
1 tsp flaky sea salt
2 tbsp za'atar

to garnish

a large bunch of flat-leaf parsley,
   leaves picked
seeds from ½ large pomegranate
2 tbsp pine nuts, toasted (optional)

equipment

2 casserole dishes (Dutch
   ovens), one of which will
   hold your chicken
blender (or food processor)

In this Middle Eastern dish lots of amazing things – succulent poached chicken, soft confited chickpeas (I am indebted to Ottolenghi for these), tahini (but of course), fresh tomatoes and crunchy za'atar flatbread croutons – get layered up to create something spectacular. It may not be a looker (*fatteh* means 'crushed' in Arabic), but it tastes phenomenal. Don't be put off by the long list of ingredients – while this hardly qualifies as a midweek dinner, the individual components are simple to execute. This is what you would cook for a dinner party, but a relaxed one where your oldest mates are coming over.

1. Preheat the oven to 130°C fan/150°C/300°F/gas 2. Line a baking tray with baking paper.

2. Start with the confit chickpeas: combine all the ingredients in a casserole dish (Dutch oven), cover with the lid, then transfer to the oven and cook for 1 hour 15 minutes. These should be ready just in time for you to plate up.

3. Meanwhile, poach the chicken: season the bird with the allspice, olive oil, salt and several grinds of pepper. Add the lemon halves to the cavity. Place in a casserole dish that will fit the chicken snugly and cover with cold water. Place on the hob over a medium heat and bring to the boil, then reduce the heat to low and simmer gently for 1 hour until the chicken is cooked. Remove the bird from the pan and leave to cool.

4. Shred the chicken meat into a bowl, add the sumac and pomegranate molasses. Taste and adjust the seasoning, if required.

5. For the tahini yoghurt sauce, whisk together the ingredients until smooth.

6. For the tomato sauce, combine the tomatoes, chilli and cumin seeds in a blender and blitz until smooth, then gradually add the olive oil and blend again. The mixture will emulsify and the texture will go silky. Add salt to taste, then pass through a sieve (fine mesh strainer).

7. Remove the chickpeas from the oven and set aside with the lid on. Increase the oven temperature to 220°C fan/240°C/475°F/gas 9.

8. For the croutons, separate each flatbread into two halves, then layer the pieces on top of each other. Cut the bread into pieces about 4cm (1½in) square. Add these to the prepared baking tray, drizzle with a glug of olive oil and the salt, then toss together. Bake in the oven for 5–10 minutes, then remove and toss with the za'atar.

9. To serve, spread half of the tahini yoghurt sauce over a large platter. Add spoonfuls of the tomato sauce and marble this through the yoghurt. Use a slotted spoon to spoon over half of the chickpeas, then drizzle over a tablespoon of their oil. Add half of the chicken followed by half of the croutons. Repeat all the layers, then garnish with parsley and pomegranate seeds (and toasted pine nuts, if you're feeling flush).

no-churn tahini ice cream with caramelised walnuts

Serves 6-8

for the caramelised walnuts
180g (6½oz) walnuts
2 tbsp maple syrup
1½ tbsp tahini
2 tsp extra-virgin olive oil
¼ tsp fine sea salt

for the ice cream
140g (5oz/½ cup) tahini
4 tbsp Cazcabel honey tequila
   (or dark rum)
675ml (23fl oz/2¾ cups) double
   (heavy) cream
120g (4oz/1 cup) icing
   (confectioners') sugar

for the bananas (optional)
1½ tbsp coconut oil
70g (3oz/generous ¼ cup) light brown
   sugar
1½ tbsp water
4 bananas, thickly sliced

equipment
900g (2lb) loaf tin

This is wildly simple to make and one of those desserts that my friends can't stop eating. It's a sweet dessert that's just pulled back from the edge by the bitterness of the tahini, alcohol and walnuts, resulting in something altogether grown-up. The caramelised walnuts, which – I warn you – are completely addictive, are adapted from Alison Roman. Meanwhile, the brown sugar bananas, while optional, add further indulgence and make this dinner-party-worthy.

It is best to use a Middle Eastern brand of tahini for this recipe in order to get the right texture. This dessert requires freezing overnight.

1. Preheat the oven to 160°C fan/180°C/350°F/gas 4. Line the loaf tin with cling film (plastic wrap) with a decent overhang on each side. Line a baking tray with baking paper.

2. Spread the walnuts over the baking tray, then coat with the maple syrup, tahini, olive oil and salt. Roast in the oven for 12–15 minutes – use your nose with this one, you will start to smell when things are starting to get toasty – then remove from the oven and leave to cool. Once cool, set a quarter aside in an airtight container and lightly crush the rest.

3. To make the ice cream, whisk together the tahini and tequila in a medium bowl – the mixture may seize up, but don't worry.

4. In a separate bowl (and with a clean whisk), whip the double cream and icing sugar to soft peaks. Add a spoonful or two of the cream into the tahini mix and whisk to loosen up the tahini mixture. Fold in the rest of the cream until the mixture is smooth and uniform, followed by the crushed caramelised walnuts.

5. Pour the mixture into the prepared loaf tin, top with a square of baking paper and fold the overhanging cling film over the top. Freeze overnight.

6. Make the brown sugar bananas just before serving. Melt the coconut oil in a medium pan over a medium heat, then add the light brown sugar and water and cook until slightly syrupy and bubbling. Add the sliced bananas and cook for around 5 minutes until the bananas have started to soften and everything is caramelised.

7. To serve, turn the ice cream cake out, remove the cling film and slice into portions. Spoon over the brown sugar bananas (if using), scatter over the reserved caramelised walnuts and serve.

beer

Beer is one of the world's most popular drinks (only tea and water surpass it), but it has yet to count me as a loyal drinker. Perhaps this speaks to the fact that there is no one type of bitterness: you can be obsessed with grapefruit, coffee and cocoa, yet wince when sipping a pint. Truthfully, researching beer for this chapter has been my first proper introduction to the drink – and it's been both delicious and disorientating. A dizzying number of beers exist: all manner of ales and lagers, porters, stouts, wheat beers, sub-categories within sub-categories. Initially I yearned for the comparative simplicity of wine classification, where it's white or red, possibly rosé, occasionally orange and hopefully fizzy . . . Beer doesn't feel as neat and, in a way, therein lies its beauty: it is complex in terms of categorisation, history, taste and aroma. It can be deep, subtle, dark, light, malty, toasty, bitter, sweet. It's a whole world of flavour.

Taking it back to basics, here's my beer 101. All beers sort into two main categories: ales and lagers. Ales are fermented for a short period at warm temperatures using top-fermenting yeasts (quite literally, what it says on the tin). Lagers are fermented for a longer period at cooler temperatures using bottom-fermenting yeasts. The ale category is where you'll find a lot of recognisable sub-categories, ranging from light to heavy: blonde ales, pale ales, real ales, brown ales, porters and stouts. Meanwhile, in the lager category you have pale, Vienna and dark lagers, beyond which you get into varieties that originate from specific locations, often in Germany, such as Pilsner, Märzen, Doppelbock and Dunkel.

The brewing process involves boiling, fermentation and blending. When handling bitterness we often seek to balance out or counteract it with something softer: such as when we combine cocoa solids with cocoa butter, milk and sugar to give us easy-going milk chocolate. But with beer, the brewing process seeks to *unearth* bitterness rather than temper it: hops undergo boiling specifically to extract the alpha acids that make beer bitter – in other words, bitterness is the point. So, how did we come to be so universally attached to this bitter drink? The answer lies in the history books.

Beer has been brewed for thousands of years, not only because it is pleasantly mood-altering but, crucially, because it is safe to drink and calorific. Drinking alcohol daily was a common practice between the fourteenth and eighteenth centuries because water was often diseased and the production of alcohol killed viruses and bacteria, thereby making it a safer drinking option. Incidentally, in Asia they chose to simply brew tea over brewing alcohol, hence the respective tea- vs beer-drinking cultures in the East and West (not sure what that says about us). Beyond the safety aspect, fermented drinks have long been a source of sustenance, which was no doubt the inspiration behind Guinness's 1920s slogan 'Guinness is good for you' – a statement that would never pass today. Still, you wouldn't be wrong to consider beer as liquid bread, insofar as it offers carbs, a few B vitamins and potassium.

It turns out that brewing was originally a female activity – a *wifely* one, even. Back in medieval times it was a traditional household responsibility to brew ale to feed a family. In fact, alcohol was brewed from all sorts: honey, grains, flowers, herbs. This subsequently morphed into a relatively lucrative and stable trade for women in England, with the term 'alewife' describing a woman who brewed ale for commercial sale. It was not to last, however. With the Industrial Revolution came the commercialisation of brewing and, by the end of the nineteenth century, women no longer featured (a familiar tale). Today, the brewing industry is worth billions globally, and women have a very small stake (steak!) in the ale pie. Women used to create unique brews out of necessity – that is, with what was available – and now, with the modern craft beer movement, we find ourselves full circle. These days, to be a woman brewer, winemaker or distiller is to be a pioneer – the ultimate irony.

Beyond the making of beer, there's the drinking of it. And although I do generally focus – unapologetically – on what I like to eat, it's true that getting to grips with an ingredient or style of food that isn't to your taste can spark creativity in the kitchen. Experimenting with beer has truly broadened my culinary horizons: who knew that I would love crêpes made with lager so much (page 112)? That Guinness and cheese would be such a dreamy combination (page 106)? That my ragu made with a London Porter (as opposed to my usual go-to, red wine) would end up being the dish my friends have liked more than any other I've ever made (page 108)? I hope you enjoy the recipes in this chapter: the inclusion of beer serves to add a slight edge or ferrous tang (as Nigella has often evocatively described it), but these recipes are, at their core, all about comfort – and that, I feel, has universal appeal.

rye, pear + maple porridge

Serves 2

200g (7oz) rye bread (stale or fresh),
    crusts removed
150ml (5fl oz/⅔ cup) London Porter
    (or stout)
320ml (11fl oz/generous 1¼ cups)
    water
2 tbsp maple syrup (if you really like
    unusual/tangy/bitter flavours –
    like me! – reduce this to 1 tbsp)
½ tsp ground nutmeg
¼ tsp ground cardamom
½ tsp ground cinnamon
1 tsp vanilla bean paste
zest and juice of ½ orange
½ tsp flaky sea salt

to serve

1 fresh pear, peeled and sliced
Greek yoghurt (or coconut yoghurt,
    to keep it vegan)
maple syrup

TIP

The key to getting a good,
creamy texture when making
porridge (including the
traditional oat-based kind) is
to soak your grains 30 minutes
before you plan to cook them
(or overnight, if it's easier).
This doesn't apply to 'quick-
cook' oats.

Across cultures, some of the most delicious dishes have started with the thrifty need to use up stale bread: French *pain perdu*, Tuscan *ribollita*, British bread and butter pudding, Middle Eastern *fattoush* . . . And this breakfast – *ollenbrød* (which translates as 'beer bread') – is the Danes' version: a tangy, bitter, complex 'porridge' made of stale rye bread and beer.

I'll call it: this one is going to be polarising, but I first came across it in Copenhagen and instantly fell in love with its deep, spiced flavour, which is perfect in the winter months. It's not mild like the porridge we're familiar with – it's intense, malty, a bit sour, a bit salty – but it is extremely comforting and delicious. Do not skip the pear, yoghurt or maple syrup on top: all three balance out the porridge's unusual flavours.

This recipe requires you to soak the bread in advance, so do factor this in when making.

1. Tear the rye bread into smallish pieces and place in a medium saucepan. Pour over the beer and leave to soak for a couple of hours (or overnight).

2. To cook the porridge, add the rest of the ingredients to the pan, stir and then set over a medium-high heat to bring the mixture to the boil. Reduce the heat to medium-low and let the porridge bubble away for 15–20 minutes, stirring regularly to break up the bread, until it reaches a thick porridge consistency.

3. Divide between two bowls and top each with half a pear, a spoonful of Greek yoghurt and a drizzle of maple syrup. Leave the yoghurt and maple syrup on the table for top-ups.

curry leaf mussels with indian lager

Serves 2

1 ice cube
2–3 pinches of saffron threads,
    ground in a pestle and mortar
1kg (2lb 4oz) mussels
50g (2oz) butter
2 leeks, quartered lengthways,
    then sliced crossways about
    1cm (½in) thick
3 bay leaves
fine sea salt
3 garlic cloves, crushed
1½ tbsp curry powder
25 fresh (or dried) curry leaves
1 tsp mustard seeds
200ml (7fl oz/scant 1 cup) Indian
    lager, such as Cobra or Kingfisher
    (or a gluten-free lager)
200ml (7fl oz/scant 1 cup) coconut
    milk
freshly ground black pepper
small handful of coriander (cilantro)
    or flat-leaf parsley, finely
    chopped, to serve

This started as a twist on French *mouclade* – the lesser-known cousin of *moules marinière* – which combines mussels with a creamy, curried sauce. But it has become a *mouclade* that has started to reclaim its roots: with Indian lager in place of white wine, a handful of curry leaves (for incredible fragrance) and coconut milk in place of cream.

When cooking mussels it is best to get your ingredients fully prepped before you start. And although this dish does require a degree of last-minute cooking, it's perfect for an easy, budget-conscious supper with friends. Best served with crusty bread or fries (or both!).

1. About 30 minutes before cooking, place an ice cube in a small bowl and sprinkle over the ground saffron. Set aside, allowing it to melt. This produces a vibrant, aromatic saffron concentrate.

2. Meanwhile, rinse and clean the mussels, removing any beards and discarding any that have broken shells or remain open.

3. Melt the butter in a heavy-based pan until foaming. Reduce the heat to medium-low and add the leeks, bay leaves and half a teaspoon of fine sea salt. Cook gently until soft but not coloured, around 10 minutes. Add the garlic, curry powder, curry leaves and mustard seeds, then cook for another 2 minutes until everything is smelling fragrant. Stir in the saffron concentrate and leave on the lowest heat possible.

4. Before cooking the mussels, have a large bowl ready by the side of the stove. Add the mussels to a large pan, cover with a lid, and cook over a medium-high heat for around 3 minutes, shaking the pan occasionally. Pour over the lager, then replace the lid and cook for another 2 minutes. Use tongs or a slotted spoon to remove the mussels that have opened to the waiting bowl. Replace the lid for another minute or so, until all the mussels have opened. Discard any that do not open.

5. Once the mussels are cooked, you'll have some liquor left in the bottom of the pan, which will be a mix of the mussel juices and lager. If this looks murky or gritty, then strain it through a fine mesh strainer or piece of muslin (cheesecloth) directly into the curry sauce. Wipe out the mussel pan, add the mussels back, cover with the lid to keep them warm and set aside, off the heat.

6. Simmer the sauce until reduced by half, then add the coconut milk and simmer for a further couple of minutes until thickened slightly. Add more salt to taste and a couple of grinds of black pepper. Pour the sauce over the mussels, scatter over the coriander, then bring the pot to the table.

roast chicken with beer butter onions

Serves 3-4

1 whole chicken (around 1.5kg/3lb)
1 tbsp Diamond kosher salt
freshly ground black pepper
150ml (5fl oz/⅔ cup) IPA
150ml (5fl oz/⅔ cup) olive oil
2 garlic cloves, crushed
2 tsp flaky sea salt
6 large (or 8 small) banana shallots,
    peeled and halved lengthways
2–3 fresh thyme sprigs

This is a wonderfully low-effort but flavourful one-pot dish that works just as well for a weeknight meal as it does for a weekend feast. I like it served with crusty bread or potatoes to soak up the juices and some wilted greens or a green salad with a lemony dressing and shavings of Parmesan.

I use the word 'butter' loosely here – as you'll notice, there isn't actually any butter in this dish, but the shallots, once cooked, become so soft and unctuous that you could reasonably describe them as 'like butter'.

1. Preheat the oven to 200°C fan/220°C/425°F/gas 7.

2. Prepare the chicken by drying it thoroughly, then season with the kosher salt and a few grinds of black pepper. Set aside.

3. In a large cast-iron pot (Dutch oven), whisk together the IPA, olive oil, garlic and flaky sea salt. Add the shallots and thyme. Place the chicken on top of the shallots and roast in the oven for 1 hour until the shallots are soft and starting to caramelise, and the chicken is golden brown. The juices should run clear when a knife or skewer is poked into the thickest part of the chicken.

4. Remove from the oven and allow to rest for 20 minutes, then carve up the chicken and serve alongside the shallots.

TIP

Preparing the chicken in this way is called dry brining, and it is the secret to a chicken that is juicy and seasoned throughout. It works even better when you season the chicken the night before you plan to cook it.

rarebit mac'n'cheese

Serves 4 as a main or 8 as a side

60g (2½oz) butter
60g (2½oz/½ cup) plain (all-purpose)
    flour
1 x 440ml (15fl oz) bottle of Guinness
    (or another stout)
100ml (3½fl oz/scant ½ cup) whole
    milk
500g (1lb 2oz) mature Cheddar,
    grated
100g (3½oz) Parmesan, grated
2 tbsp Worcestershire sauce
1 tsp hot paprika
½ tsp cayenne pepper (optional)
freshly ground black pepper
400g (14oz) macaroni pasta
Diamond kosher salt
10 sage leaves (optional)

equipment
31 x 25cm (12 x 10in) baking dish

MAKE AHEAD
You can make this up to
24 hours ahead of baking
and store it in the fridge.

Mac'n'cheese offers unadulterated comfort: it is milky and silky, cheesy and soft. There's absolutely nothing challenging about it – except perhaps its health credentials (but let's not dwell). In this version, I invite you to make your cheese sauce with stout – as in Welsh rarebit (aka posh cheese on toast) – because it imparts a savouriness that makes this particularly moreish.

1. Preheat the oven to 180°C fan/200°C/400°F/gas 6.

2. Melt the butter in a pan over a medium–low heat, then add the flour and stir until a thick paste forms. Cook out the flour for 4–5 minutes, then gradually add the Guinness, whisking as you go until you have a thick, smooth sauce. Gradually add the milk, followed by three-quarters of the Cheddar, all of the Parmesan, the Worcestershire sauce, paprika, cayenne pepper (if using) and a good grind or two of black pepper. Stir until the cheese is fully melted. The texture should be thicker than double (heavy) cream but still very pourable. Leave the sauce over a very low heat until you're ready to use it.

3. Part-cook the pasta for 6 minutes in well-salted water (see Tip). Just before draining, scoop out a mugful of the pasta water and set aside.

4. Stir the drained pasta into the rarebit sauce and stir in some of the reserved pasta water until it's your desired thickness (bearing in mind that the pasta will absorb more sauce while it bakes in the oven). Transfer to the baking dish and top with the remaining Cheddar, followed by the sage leaves. Bake until golden and bubbling, around 25 minutes.

TIP
This is a good ratio to remember when cooking pasta: 1 litre (1 quart) of water to 1 tbsp Diamond kosher salt to 100g (3½oz) pasta.

porter beef shin ragu with parmesan orzo

Serves 6

3 tbsp cornflour (cornstarch)
fine sea salt and freshly ground
    black pepper
1kg (2lb 4oz) beef shin, bone-in (or ¾
    boneless beef shin plus ¼ oxtail)
vegetable oil
100g (3½oz) pancetta, cubed
2 banana shallots (or 3 standard
    shallots), finely chopped
2 medium carrots, finely chopped
2 celery sticks, finely chopped
200ml (7fl oz/scant 1 cup) whole milk
½ bottle of London Porter (about
    250ml/8½fl oz)
1 x 400g (14oz) tin plum tomatoes
1 tbsp white balsamic vinegar (or 1½
    tsp balsamic vinegar), or to taste
1 tsp flaky sea salt, or as needed

for the parmesan orzo

1 ice cube
2 pinches of saffron, ground in a
    pestle and mortar
500g (1lb 2oz) orzo
100ml (3½fl oz/scant ½ cup) double
    (heavy) cream
100g (3½oz) Parmesan, finely grated,
    plus extra to serve
25g (1oz) butter

TIP

Using a cartouche when slow-
cooking helps ensure that
whatever you're making cooks
uniformly.

MAKE AHEAD

You can make the ragu the day
before you want to serve it – in
fact, it would be improved for it.

This is comfort food at its very best. It's something to make for your real friends: the ones you don't need to impress with pretty plates, but who will appreciate the simplicity and sheer deliciousness of this dish. When I made it for my tribe, every single bowl was scraped clean (which is always the real feedback that us cooks look for). The beer offers depth of flavour, and while you might feel that the addition of milk is rogue, it brings the bitter and acidic notes of the beer and tomatoes into balance, resulting in harmony. Plus, this easy twist on *risotto alla Milanese* – inspired by chef Mike Davies – makes a mild, creamy, comforting partner to the depth of the ragu.

1. Preheat the oven to 130°C fan/150°C/300°F/gas 2.

2. Place the cornflour on a plate, season generously with salt and pepper, then dust the beef shin pieces in the cornflour.

3. Set a casserole dish (Dutch oven) over a medium–high heat. When hot, add a thin layer of vegetable oil and sear the beef in batches, ensuring all-over caramelisation, then remove from the pan. Add a small splash of water to the pan to deglaze it, then reduce the heat and add the pancetta, allowing it to cook until lightly golden, around 5 minutes.

4. Add the shallots, carrot and celery, and cook for 10–15 minutes until softened. If needed, add a little more vegetable oil. When the vegetables are cooked, nestle the beef pieces in among them, turn the heat up slightly and add the milk, letting it reduce by half. Add the porter and tomatoes, then place a cartouche (a circle of baking paper with a small hole in the middle) on top, followed by the casserole lid. Cook in the oven for 4–5 hours until the meat is falling off the bone. Add the white balsamic vinegar, as well as salt, to taste.

5. Bloom the saffron: place an ice cube in a small bowl and sprinkle over the ground saffron. Set aside, allowing the ice cube to melt.

6. Cook the pasta in well-salted water according to the packet instructions. Reserve half a mugful of the starchy cooking water, then drain. Return the drained pasta to the pan along with the saffron concentrate, cream and reserved pasta water, stirring until the sauce emulsifies. Take off the heat and fold in the Parmesan and butter until melted – in consistency it should look and feel like a good risotto: silky smooth and reasonably loose.

7. To serve, ladle the orzo into bowls, then top it with the ragu and a generous shower of Parmesan.

stout sticky toffee pudding

Makes 6

100g (3½oz) butter, browned, plus
    extra for greasing
200g (7oz) Medjool dates, stones
    removed, torn into pieces
125ml (4fl oz/½ cup) dark rum
    (Mount Gay works well here)
    or boiling water
90g (3½oz/scant ½ cup) dark
    muscovado sugar
175g (6oz/generous 1¼ cups) self-
    raising flour
1 tsp baking powder
½ tsp fine sea salt
2 eggs
75ml (3fl oz/⅓ cup) whole milk
1 tbsp treacle
1 tsp vanilla bean paste

for the sauce
250g (9oz) butter
250g (9oz/1¼ cups) light muscovado
    sugar
250ml (8½fl oz/1 cup) double
    (heavy) cream
150ml (5fl oz/ generous ½ cup)
    London Porter

to serve
vanilla ice cream

equipment
6 dariole moulds or ramekins (around
    220ml/8fl oz capacity)

TIP
Incorporating browned butter
into cakes is a great way of
adding depth of flavour. It works
especially well with autumnal
and winter flavours – think
caramel, nuts and sweet spices.
See also: Cranberry Brown
Butter Bakewells (page 148).

This was inspired by a knockout pudding I ate at The Harwood Arms in London: a malted treacle tart with a stout caramel sauce. That sauce! I had to find a way to use it – and, in this very British pud, its subtle bitterness takes the already perfect sticky toffee pudding (STP) to the next level. Allow me to introduce you to the SSTP. It is mandatory that you serve it thus: top each SSTP with a ball of vanilla ice cream and pour the caramel sauce over the top.

(PS Beer experts: I know that a London Porter isn't technically a stout, but please allow me the satisfaction of alliteration here!)

1. Preheat the oven to 180°C fan/200°C/400°F/gas 6 and butter the dariole moulds or ramekins.

2. Place the dates and rum in a pan, bring to the boil, then turn off the heat. Use a fork to mash the dates into a rough paste and set aside.

3. Place the sugar, flour, baking powder and salt in a medium to large mixing bowl and whisk together until combined, using your hands to break up any lumps of sugar.

4. In a separate jug or bowl, whisk together the butter, eggs, milk, treacle, vanilla and mashed dates, then add these to the dry ingredients and whisk just until you have a homogenous batter.

5. Divide the mixture equally among the dariole moulds, then bake in the oven for 20–22 minutes until an inserted skewer comes out clean.

6. Leave to cool for around 5 minutes before releasing them from the moulds. Slice the domes off to ensure a level base.

7. For the caramel sauce, melt the butter and sugar together over a medium heat, whisking frequently as it starts to bubble. After 3 or so minutes the sugar should have melted fully and the mixture will be thick. Take the pan off the heat, allow to cool for a minute, then whisk in the double cream. If you've used unsalted butter add a pinch or two of sea salt flakes at this point as well. Put the pan back on the heat and bubble away for 2 minutes, whisking regularly. Next, add the London Porter and then let the sauce bubble away for 10 minutes, whisking regularly, until slightly thickened and glossy. (If your sauce splits, whisk in a tablespoon of freshly boiled water – this should bring it back together.) Serve the sticky toffee puddings in shallow bowls, topped with a scoop of vanilla ice cream and covered in a generous quantity of the caramel sauce.

malted crêpes with lime + sugar

Makes around 16

1 tbsp malt extract (or honey)
100ml (3½fl oz/scant ½ cup) milk
250ml (8½fl oz/generous 1 cup)
    Corona beer
50ml (2fl oz/3 tbsp plus 1 tsp) double
    (heavy) cream
3 eggs
240g (9oz/scant 2 cups) plain
    (all-purpose) flour
2 tbsp granulated sugar
½ tsp fine sea salt
40g (1½oz) butter, plus extra
    for cooking

to serve
limes
granulated sugar

This Corona beer-related creation is a very happy one, with the beer bringing a subtle malty flavour to these otherwise classic French crêpes. I serve this with fresh lime and sugar not just because a Corona beer is usually stoppered with a wedge of lime, but also because this green citrus has all the sourness of lemon while also offering up an extra floral quality.

It's not essential, but if you can factor in time to rest the batter for an hour (or overnight) your crêpes will be even better, as you'll be giving the flour time to absorb the liquid properly.

1. In a large jug, combine the malt extract with a splash or two of the milk and whisk together until homogenous, then whisk in the rest of the milk, beer, cream and eggs until well combined.

2. In a medium bowl, whisk together the flour, sugar and salt. Make a well in the middle of the flour mixture and add half of the liquid, whisking thoroughly until there are no lumps. Gradually add the rest of the liquid, whisking as you go until fully incorporated. The batter should be the consistency of double (heavy) cream. Pour the crêpe batter back into the large jug that you measured your wet ingredients into and set aside to rest for at least 15 minutes.

3. When you're ready to cook the pancakes, set a non-stick crêpe pan or frying pan (skillet) over a gentle heat. Add the butter and allow it to melt, then pour this into your pancake batter and give it a very brief whisk to incorporate (it's important that the butter is not too hot).

4. Turn the heat up under your pan and allow it to get hot (crêpes are best cooked quickly on a relatively high heat, with a small amount of fat). Use kitchen paper to wipe out any excess butter. Pour a small quantity (about 60ml/2fl oz/¼ cup) of the batter into the pan and swirl it around until the bottom of the pan is evenly coated. Cook until the edges start to come away and it has some golden colour on the underside (you can lift a bit up to check). Flip the pancake with a palette knife or by tossing it. Cook the other side for around 30 seconds, then slide out of the pan and onto a plate. The first one always looks rubbish but still tastes nice – chef's treat.

5. Lightly grease the pan before repeating with the next pancake.

6. Serve with the lime wedges and granulated sugar.

great-gran's christmas pudding

Serves 8-10

This is closely related to the Christmas pudding of Violet Tanswell, my great-great-grandmother and the mother of the original Alexina, who I am named after. Violet's Christmas pudding is the basis of the recipe we use every year in our house and I doubt things will ever change. I know a contingent of people do not like Christmas pudding, but this is not a group that I identify with. I am obsessed with the stuff, especially this one – perhaps because you only get to eat it once a year.

This is truly superior made a year in advance – it's great to get into a habit of being a year ahead (each Christmas, make your pudding for the next year) – but at the very least, make it 2–3 months before Christmas: time is essential in helping the flavours develop and harmonise.

1. In a bowl, whisk together the suet, flour, breadcrumbs, sugar, spices and salt. Stir through the dried fruit, followed by the grated apple and carrot.

2. Separately, whisk together the egg, stout, zests and orange juice in a large jug. Fold this mixture into the dry ingredients until well-combined. The mixture should look moist but feel relatively stiff.

3. Transfer the mixture to your pudding basin, packing it tight, then level off the top and cover with a disc of greaseproof paper. Cover with a tea towel and place in a cool, dark place and leave to mature for 2 to 3 days – you'll see the mixture darken over this time.

4. After resting, prepare the pudding with greaseproof paper, foil and string (it is easiest to watch a YouTube tutorial for this), then steam the pudding for around 6 hours (I do this in a large saucepan with an upturned saucer in the bottom). Keep a regular eye on the water level and top up with boiling water as needed.

5. Remove the pudding from the steamer and let it go completely cold. Rewrap with fresh greaseproof paper, foil and string, then store the pudding for 2–3 months (or up to a year) in a cool, dry place.

6. On Christmas Day, steam the pudding for 1–2 hours, again keeping an eye on the water level.

7. To serve, remove the pudding from the steamer and take off the wrapping. Slide a palette knife all around the pudding and turn it out onto a warmed plate. Serve with brandy butter, brandy sauce or cream – or all three (I have been known to).

170g (6oz/generous ⅓ cup) suet, shredded
75g (3oz/scant ¾ cup) self-raising flour
75g (3oz/1 cup) breadcrumbs
75g (3oz/scant ½ cup) light muscovado (or soft light brown) sugar
½ tsp ground nutmeg
½ tsp ground ginger
½ tsp ground allspice
½ tsp fine sea salt
75g (3oz/generous ½ cup) raisins
75g (3oz/generous ½ cup) sultanas
25g mixed peel
75g (3oz/scant ¾ cup) currants
1 small cooking apple, grated
½ medium carrot, grated
1 egg, beaten
100ml (3 ½fl oz/scant ½ cup) stout
zest of ½ lemon
zest and juice of ½ orange

equipment
1 x 18cm pudding basin (around 1.5–1.7 litres/3 pints capacity)

TIP
Family recipes always taste better, because nothing beats the power of memories and nostalgia.

jamaican guinness punch

Serves 2

125ml (4fl oz/½ cup) Guinness
190ml (6½fl oz/generous ¾ cup)
    whole milk (or unsweetened
    almond milk)
½ tsp vanilla bean paste
pinch of ground nutmeg
pinch of ground cinnamon
60ml (2fl oz/¼ cup) condensed milk
ice, to serve

equipment
blender (ideal, but not esssential)

Guinness punch is a drink that's very dear to Jamaicans (although you can find it all over the Caribbean) and present at most family gatherings – particularly on Sundays. If you like Baileys but your tastes also skew to bitter, then this is the drink for you. It's cold, creamy and comforting with the sweet notes of cinnamon, nutmeg and vanilla, but I'm convinced it's the bitterness of the Guinness that makes you go back for more.

This can easily be made vegan by substituting the whole milk for unsweetened almond milk and the condensed milk for vegan condensed milk (Carnation do a great version).

1. Add the ingredients to a blender and whizz briefly (or you can whisk everything together by hand).

2. Pour over ice to serve.

walnuts

The wrinkly, brain-shaped walnut is pecan's old-fashioned, bitter cousin and the world's second most popular nut. In some ways, pecans and walnuts are interchangeable, but the added complexity of walnuts makes them more versatile. Most bitter ingredients are strong in flavour, but walnuts are on the milder side, with just a 'hint of nicotine bitterness', as Niki Segnit (author of *The Flavour Thesaurus*) so beautifully puts it. It is the process of kiln-drying that brings out their mildly tannic nature, but this is concentrated in the skin of the walnut, rather than in the nut itself, which is sweeter. Toasting brings out their full flavour, but forget about a batch in the oven (we've all been there) and it quickly goes too far: charred walnuts are a notable example of bitter on bitter (see page 21) that I would probably not recommend!

Walnuts have a timeless quality; they remind me of grandfathers, forests, roaring fires and tobacco. Accordingly, the walnut tree is the oldest tree known to man (cultivation began in 7000 BC) and it takes time to grow: a seedling walnut tree won't fruit until it is at least 10–15 years old. They need sun and shelter and are territorial: other plants are less likely to grow under them because the fallen leaves of the walnut tree contain a natural herbicide. The variety most widely cultivated worldwide is the English walnut, also known (more accurately) as the Persian walnut. This variety seems to have originated in Asia Minor but today most of the world's walnuts are produced by China, followed by the US.

Although walnuts don't have the current cool of almonds, the sweetness of pecans or the regal quality of pistachios, they are one of the most versatile nuts in the kitchen. Their bitterness makes them good with fatty meats, but their own meaty, firm and slightly waxy texture also makes them a useful ingredient for plant-based foods, where they add richness, body and creaminess. More broadly, you'll find that walnuts and garlic appear everywhere across the Med: in Italian *salsa di noci*, *aillade* from the Languedoc region in France, and *tarator* from Turkey.

In the realm of cakes and desserts, walnuts like sticky autumnal flavours and spices – maple, cinnamon, nutmeg – as well as intensely fudgy dried fruits. Try a walnut sandwiched in a Medjool date as a less indulgent substitute for a pecan pie, or the romantic Provençal poor man's nougat: a walnut enclosed in a fig and dried out in the sun. Dark chocolate, vanilla, coffee, cinnamon, sesame, caramel, candied oranges: all of these sweet but complex flavours marry beautifully with walnuts.

That walnuts bear a resemblance to the human brain likely explains why they have long been touted as brain food. Way back when, the medieval Doctrine of Signatures attributed therapeutic properties to plants based on their resemblance to specific parts of the human body and, as such, recommended walnuts for treating headaches and mental illness. This is highly debatable today, but what we do know is that walnuts are the only nut significantly high in omega 3, which makes them good for heart health, and they have been reported to have cognitive benefits, too – particularly for older generations.

The walnuts we get year-round are brown and dried, but fresh walnuts are green and, used in this precious state, make a handful of other products: *nocino* (green walnut liqueur) and the deepest, darkest pickled walnuts that became fashionable in England in the eighteenth century. In the US, you also come across black walnuts, which seem to be a different beast entirely: both far more savoury and umami-forward, and yet also sweeter. I have been known to search for the fanciest of walnut oils from delicatessens, because they make a truly delicious dressing (see the Walnut Caesar Salad on page 124). However, as these oils quickly go rancid, it is generally best to buy the whole nuts, as and when you need them. (Top tip: Lidl sells the best nuts in the UK.)

french chicory, roquefort + walnut salad

Serves 2-3

75g (3oz) walnut halves
250g (9oz) white chicory leaves,
  separated
100g (3½oz) blue cheese (I love
  Roquefort best here)
5g (¼oz) chives, finely chopped

for the dressing
couple of pinches of fine sea salt
1 tsp Dijon mustard
1 tsp honey
2 tbsp sherry (or red wine) vinegar
2 tbsp extra-virgin olive oil
4 tbsp vegetable (or sunflower) oil
freshly ground black pepper

This is one of those classic, perfect combinations, which I have fond memories of eating in France. Despite the reputation of French *haute cuisine*, with all its 'refinement' and process, in day-to-day cooking the French really nail the simple things – like the Italians, they are precious about their ingredients and see no need to over-embellish. This salad is so much greater than the sum of its parts, incredibly moreish and easy to make. If you haven't had it before, then I urge you to try it. It works beautifully in so many contexts: as a light but satiating lunch, as a punchy starter or alongside fatty meats, such as duck or pork. And the French dressing here – a Felicity Cloake recipe – is a fantastic one to have in your repertoire.

1. Preheat the oven to 160°C fan/180°C/350°F/gas 4.

2. Toast the walnuts on a baking tray in the oven for 10 minutes, then set aside to cool.

3. Meanwhile, make the dressing by adding the salt, mustard, honey and vinegar to a jam jar and shaking until combined. Add the oils, then shake again until emulsified. Season with black pepper, to taste.

4. Place the chicory leaves in a serving bowl, pour over the dressing and toss until the leaves are coated. Roughly crumble the toasted walnuts over the top with your fingers – you want some bits to be smaller and some to be larger. Crumble over the blue cheese (again, it's fine for the pieces to be uneven in size) and finish by sprinkling over the chives. Serve immediately.

orecchiette with walnuts, brown butter + brussels sprouts

Serves 2

60g (2½oz) walnuts
200g (7oz) Brussels sprouts
150g (5oz) orecchiette (or another
 type of pasta)
90g (3¼oz) butter
1 garlic clove, slightly crushed with
 the side of a knife (but kept
 whole)
fine sea salt
20g (¾oz) pecorino (or Parmesan),
 finely grated
squeeze of fresh lemon juice
handful of fresh basil leaves
freshly ground black pepper

Would I normally ask you to individually separate the leaves from Brussels sprouts? No. It's the sort of job that gets lumped in with podding broad beans for me: basically, I'd rather not. But truly, there is something so visually poetic about the way that the shape of the orecchiette ('little ears') is mirrored by the leaves of the Brussels sprouts in this dish. It's a stunner! And beyond the visual appeal there is the flavour, which is knockout and perfect for the autumn/winter season: we're talking toasty, rich brown butter; salty, umami pecorino; vegetal, subtly bitter Brussels sprouts; further toasty, bitter notes from the walnuts and aniseed freshness from the basil.

This is adapted from a recipe by one of my favourite food bloggers and authors, Alexandra Stafford.

1. Preheat the oven to 160°C fan/180°C/350°F/gas 4.

2. Toast the walnuts on a baking tray in the oven for 10 minutes. Let them cool slightly, then crush roughly using your hands.

3. Trim the bases on your Brussels sprouts and then separate them into individual leaves. Put your favourite song on and get in the zone with this task, it'll be over before you know it! Once you get to the core and it becomes hard to separate individual leaves, set aside and finely slice the cores at the end.

4. Put a pan of well-salted water on to boil for your pasta (see Tip). Add the orecchiette to the boiling water and cook for 1 minute less than the packet instructions, then drain.

5. Meanwhile, melt the butter in a frying pan (skillet) over a medium heat. Add the garlic clove to help flavour the butter and allow it to start to brown – take it to the point where it smells toasty and looks a deep golden brown (don't be scared to take this quite far), then remove the garlic clove. Add the Brussels sprouts, briefly pan-frying these for a minute or so with a pinch or two of salt. Reduce the heat to medium-low, then add the drained pasta, the toasted, crushed walnuts, half of the cheese and a small squeeze of fresh lemon. Toss everything together.

6. Serve immediately, garnished with the remaining cheese, the basil leaves and several grindings of black pepper.

TIP

This is a good ratio to remember when cooking pasta: 1 litre (1 quart) of water to 1 tbsp Diamond kosher salt to 100g (3½oz) pasta.

walnut caesar salad

Serves 2-3

75g (3oz) walnut halves
1 egg, at room temperature
½ small garlic clove, grated
zest and juice of ½ small lemon
2 anchovy fillets, mashed to a paste
    with the side of a knife
½ tsp Dijon (or wholegrain) mustard
3 tbsp vegetable oil
3 tbsp walnut oil (or olive oil)
40g (1½oz) Parmesan, grated
½ tsp Worcestershire sauce
pinch of fine sea salt
freshly ground black pepper
2 sweet cos lettuces, washed and
    spun/dried

I love the classic Caesar salad as much as the next person, but this one featuring walnuts is an equally delicious – and gluten-free – proposition. I understand that the concept of a Caesar salad without bread might seem like a sacrilege (and second best), but hear me out. The mayonnaise is made with walnut oil and the toasted walnuts make the most wonderful 'croutons', offering toastiness, crunchiness and a little welcome bitterness. This is adapted from Molly Baz's infamous 'cae-sal' and it's very moreish.

1. Preheat the oven to 160°C fan/180°C/350°F/gas 4.

2. Toast the walnuts on a baking tray in the oven for 10 minutes, then set aside.

3. Meanwhile, place a medium-large bowl on a tea (dish) towel on a kitchen surface (to stop it moving when you whisk). Use a balloon whisk to combine the egg, garlic, lemon zest and juice, anchovies and mustard. Slowly add the vegetable oil in a very thin drizzle, while whisking vigorously with the other hand. Follow this with the walnut oil – it should thicken into an emulsified dressing. Finally, whisk in half of the Parmesan, the Worcestershire sauce, salt and around 10 grinds of black pepper. Check the seasoning and adjust to taste.

4. Roughly tear the lettuce leaves into 5cm (2in) pieces directly into the dressing bowl along with half of the toasted walnuts, then toss to coat thoroughly. Sprinkle over the remaining Parmesan and the rest of the walnuts, then serve.

TIP
When working with mixtures that can split (mayonnaise, in this case), they can often be saved by whisking in 1–2 tbsp of freshly boiled water.

watercress + walnut linguine

Serves 2-3

The great thing about pesto is that it's more of a formula than anything; you can use up any greens or nuts that you have lying around. This is a slightly bitter, more complex twist to a dish that most of us have had a million times (but still love): pesto pasta. The peppery bitterness of the watercress against the toasty subtle bitterness of walnuts gives this pesto a bit more punch.

1. Cook the linguine in the boiling water seasoned with the kosher salt according to the instructions on the packet. Before draining the pasta, reserve 60ml (2½fl oz/¼ cup) of the cooking water.

2. Meanwhile, combine the watercress and walnuts in a food processor and pulse until coarsely chopped. Add the cheese, olive oil, salt, lemon juice, garlic and about 4 twists of black pepper and pulse again, then taste to check the consistency and seasoning. Adjust accordingly.

3. Use the pesto to dress the pasta along with a splash (or more) of the reserved pasta cooking water to create a glossy sauce. Serve immediately.

200g (7oz) linguine (or spaghetti)
2 litres (3½ pints/8 cups) boiling water
2 tbsp Diamond kosher salt

for the pesto
1 bag of watercress (about 80g/3oz)
20g (1oz) walnuts, toasted
40g (1½oz) Italian hard cheese (I like
    50% pecorino, 50% Parmesan, but
    you could do 100% Parmesan)
40ml (1½fl oz/2 tbsp plus 2 tsp) extra-
    virgin olive oil
pinch of fine sea salt
lemon juice, to taste
¼ garlic clove, grated or crushed
freshly ground black pepper

equipment
food processor

TIP
This is a good ratio to remember when cooking pasta: 1 litre (1 quart) of water to 1 tbsp Diamond kosher salt to 100g (3½oz) pasta.

blistered tomatoes with anchovy-walnut dressing

Serves 3-4

for the tomatoes

500g (1lb 2oz) baby plum tomatoes
½ tsp fine sea salt
3 tbsp extra-virgin olive oil
couple of sprigs of oregano (or
    thyme)
freshly ground black pepper
1 tbsp balsamic vinegar

for the polenta

1 tbsp butter, plus extra for greasing
90g (3¼oz/⅔ cup) coarse cornmeal
125ml (4fl oz/½ cup) milk
600ml (1 pint/2½ cups) water
¼ tsp fine sea salt, plus an extra pinch
    or two

for the dressing

25g (1oz) walnuts
1 anchovy fillet
1½ tsp sherry vinegar
½ small garlic clove, finely grated
zest of ¼ lemon
1½ tsp fresh lemon juice
3 tbsp extra-virgin olive oil
freshly ground black pepper

to serve

handful of flat-leaf parsley leaves,
    to garnish

equipment

small blender (or the small bowl of
    a food processor)
26 x 17cm (10 x 7in) baking dish, for
    the polenta

Tomatoes love being roasted – it sweetens them and intensifies their umami flavour – and the subtle bitterness of the walnuts works harmoniously against this.

This method for oven-baking polenta is a game-changer from Paula Wolfert – so much less faffy than stirring polenta on the stove.

This dish can easily be made dairy-free by replacing the butter with extra-virgin olive oil and the milk with oat milk.

1.   Preheat the oven to 200°C fan/220°C/425°F/gas 7. Spread the walnuts for the dressing on a baking tray and put them in to toast for 8–10 minutes, as the oven heats up.

2.   Add all the ingredients for the tomatoes, except the balsamic vinegar, to another baking tray and stir to combine.

3.   For the polenta, thoroughly grease the baking dish with butter, then add the rest of the ingredients and stir to combine.

4.   Place the tomatoes and polenta in the oven (tomatoes on the top shelf) and bake for 30–35 minutes, giving the polenta a stir two-thirds of the way through the cooking time. Add the balsamic vinegar to the tomatoes when you remove them from the oven.

5.   Meanwhile, make the dressing. Combine the anchovy and the sherry vinegar in a small blender and leave for a minute or two to allow the acid of the vinegar to break down the anchovy. Add the rest of the ingredients and pulse until a coarse dressing is formed.

6.   To serve, spread the polenta on a serving platter, then top with the tomatoes and their juices. Drizzle over a few spoonfuls of the dressing, then garnish with the parsley. It's best to allow this to cool slightly, so that it isn't piping hot.

allspice lamb chops
with pickled walnut ketchup

Serves 4-6 as a snack or starter

2 tsp allspice berries, toasted and
    ground to a fine powder
1 tsp ground cinnamon
1 tsp fine sea salt
1 tsp freshly ground black pepper
2 tbsp olive oil
12 lamb chops (from a rack of lamb
    – you can ask your butcher to
    cut these)

**for the pickled walnut
ketchup**
1 x 390g (13½oz) jar of pickled
    walnuts, drained and liquid
    reserved

equipment
stick blender

This pickled walnut ketchup is a trick I picked up from my fellow *MasterChef* finalist Claire Bruce (@claires_kitchentable). It couldn't be simpler: whizz up a jar of drained pickled walnuts and you have a tart, piquant condiment in seconds. As one of the richer, fattier meats out there, lamb benefits from something with this flavour profile served alongside. Allspice (a highly underrated spice) provides the flavour bridge between the two.

The lamb chops are best marinated for at least an hour.

1. Mix the spices together, then combine them with the olive oil and use to thoroughly coat the lamb chops (this is easiest to achieve by getting your hands in there). Set the lamb chops aside to marinate (ideally for an hour).

2. For the pickled walnut ketchup, blend the drained walnuts until smooth, then stir in 1½ teaspoons of the reserved pickle juice.

3. Set a large frying pan (skillet) over a medium-high heat. When hot, add half of the chops to the pan, fat-side down, and cook for 4 minutes until the fat starts to melt. Increase the heat to high and leave the chops to cook, still on the fat side, for 1 minute, then flip them over onto their sides. Cook for 1 minute (resist the urge to move them around), then flip over – both sides should have developed some colour. Transfer to a tray or plate, wipe the pan clean and repeat with the remaining chops.

4. Allow the chops to rest for a couple of minutes before serving alongside the pickled walnut ketchup.

aubergine, walnut + pomegranate *melanzane*

Serves 4-6

4 large (or 5 medium) aubergines (eggplants), sliced lengthways into 1cm (½in) thick slices
80ml (3fl oz/⅓ cup) olive oil
½ tsp fine sea salt
40g (1½oz/1 cup) panko breadcrumbs
1 tbsp extra-virgin olive oil
80g (3¼oz) Parmesan, grated
20g (¾oz) flat-leaf parsley, roughly chopped
2 tbsp capers, coarsely chopped
500g (1lb 2oz) mozzarella, drained and torn into small pieces

for the walnut and pomegranate sauce
1½ tsp plain (all-purpose) flour
200g (7oz) walnuts, blended to an uneven but fine crumb in a food processor or blender
300ml (10fl oz/1⅓ cups) vegetable stock
90ml (3fl oz/generous ⅓ cup) pomegranate molasses

for the tomato sauce
2 x 400g (14oz) tins plum tomatoes
70g (3oz) butter
1 medium white onion, peeled and halved
½ tsp fine sea salt

equipment
food processor
2–3 baking trays
stick blender (ideal, but not essential)
34 x 25cm (12 x 10in) baking dish

The brief in the penultimate round of *MasterChef* was to cook an interpretation of a classic dish and I felt it was entirely fair game to look beyond Western cuisines. I chose the Iranian classic *fesenjan* – at its core a stew of chicken (or duck), ground walnuts and pomegranate molasses – because this combination of flavours is truly otherworldly (and complex, given how few ingredients there are). You had to laugh at some of the comments on Twitter at the time, such as 'Is it really a classic if I don't recognise it?' – well yes, Chris, it is. And in the words of John, who replied to this particular keyboard warrior, 'Fortunately the world is bigger than your backyard.'

Here, I've taken an Italian vegetarian classic – *melanzane* – and included some of the flavours of *fesenjan* in the form of an earthy ground walnut and pomegranate sauce. Flat-leaf parsley and capers keep the flavours bright here, but I would also opt to serve a green salad with a lemony vinaigrette alongside.

If you can, buy a Middle Eastern brand of pomegranate molasses for this, as they tend to err more on the sour side.

1. Preheat the oven to 210°C fan/230°C/450°F/gas 8. Line the baking trays with greaseproof paper.

2. Lay the aubergine slices on the prepared baking trays, then brush with half of the olive oil. Turn the slices over and repeat, then sprinkle the salt over evenly. Roast in the oven for 30 minutes, moving the trays around halfway through to ensure they all turn evenly golden brown.

3. For the walnut and pomegranate sauce, set a medium saucepan over a medium-high heat and toast the flour until it turns a slightly darker white (or until you can smell slightly toasty notes). Add the ground walnuts and cook for 3–4 minutes, stirring often to make sure they don't catch. Add the vegetable stock and bring to the boil, then reduce the heat to a bare simmer, cover and cook for 40 minutes.

4. Separately, make the tomato sauce. Combine the tomatoes, butter, onion and salt in a heavy-based saucepan set over a medium heat and bring to a simmer. Reduce the heat and allow to simmer slowly for around 45 minutes, or until droplets of fat float free of the tomatoes, then remove the onion from the sauce. You can lightly crush the tomatoes against the sides of the pot for a chunky sauce, but I prefer to blitz it in the pan with a stick blender until completely smooth.

5. Remove the lid on the walnut pan and simmer for 20 more minutes. Next, add the pomegranate molasses and simmer for another 10 minutes until you have a dark glossy sauce/paste.

6. Toast the breadcrumbs in a pan with the extra-virgin olive oil until golden. Once cool, stir through the Parmesan, parsley and capers.

7. To assemble, spread half of the tomato sauce over the base of your baking dish. Lay half of the aubergine slices over the top (a little overlapping is good). Spread the walnut sauce over the aubergines, then sprinkle with half of the breadcrumb mixture. Arrange half of the torn mozzarella over the top. Repeat, finishing with the mozzarella.

8. Bake for 20–25 minutes. Let cool for 5–10 minutes before serving.

MAKE AHEAD

The tomato sauce, walnut sauce and breadcrumbs can be prepared up to 3 days in advance. The aubergines can be roasted the day before.

coffee + walnut *baklava*

Makes 25–30 pieces

for the walnut mixture
300g (10½oz) walnuts
¼ tsp ground cardamom
½ tsp ground cinnamon
good pinch or two of flaky sea salt

for the coffee syrup
200g (7oz/1 cup) caster (superfine)
    sugar
250ml (8½fl oz/1 cup) strong brewed
    coffee (the higher quality, the
    better)
2 cardamom pods, lightly bashed in
    a pestle and mortar
2 tsp fresh lemon juice
½ tsp vanilla bean paste

to assemble
200g (7oz) butter, melted
1 x pack of filo (phyllo) pastry
    (7 sheets, about 25 x 48cm/
    10 x 19in)

equipment
20cm (8in) square baking tin
    (or similar)
food processor
tea (dish) towel

ALTERNATIVES
I love cardamom with coffee, but coffee loves a lot of spices: you could replace the cardamom in the syrup with whole cloves or a single star anise, and the ground cardamom in the walnut mixture with ground ginger or nutmeg.

Frankly, I object to the standard story attached to *baklava*: that its intense sweetness makes it impossible to eat more than a square or two. Not if you're me. *Baklava* is sweet, but the subtle bitterness of walnuts balances that out (to some extent) and adding the robust bitterness of coffee further aids the cause. Coffee and walnut is a homely flavour combination, but in *baklava* form it's a little fancier.

Sorry to sound like a broken record, but this is much better the next day because the texture of the pastry settles and improves considerably: patience is a virtue on this occasion.

1. Preheat the oven to 160°C fan/180°C/350°F/gas 4. Place the walnuts in the dish that you're going to bake the *baklava* in and toast in the oven for around 10 minutes. Set aside to cool.

2. Meanwhile, make the coffee syrup: combine the sugar, coffee, cardamom pods and lemon juice in a pan and bring to the boil, then reduce the heat to medium and simmer gently for 15 minutes. Remove from the heat and stir in the vanilla, then strain out the cardamom pods.

3. Briefly pulse the walnuts in a food processor to a coarse crumb. Tip half of these into a bowl, then blitz the remaining nuts to a fine crumb. Add these to the bowl and stir through the spices and salt. Add in 3 tablespoons of the melted butter and stir until evenly dispersed.

4. Remove the filo from its packet and place on a board. Cut the sheets in half so you have 14 sheets, then cut down to fit your tin however you see fit. Cover with a damp tea (dish) towel.

5. Remove one filo sheet from the pile at a time and immediately replace the damp towel to prevent the rest of the pile drying out. Place the filo sheet in the tin, then brush with melted butter, leaving no dry bits. I find it easiest to spoon the melted butter onto the sheet and then use a pastry brush (or the back of the spoon) to spread it out. Build up 7 layers in this way, then add the walnut mix and spread out evenly (without pressing down) until the filo is covered. Build up another 7 layers of filo brushed with butter, then cut the *baklava* into diamond shapes (or whatever shape you prefer) with a sharp knife.

6. Bake for 1 hour until golden brown, then remove from the oven and increase the temperature to 180°C fan/200°C/400°F/gas 6. Pour the coffee syrup over the *baklava* (you might not need all of it), focusing on the lines, then return to the oven for another 5–10 minutes.

7. Leave to rest, ideally overnight in the fridge.

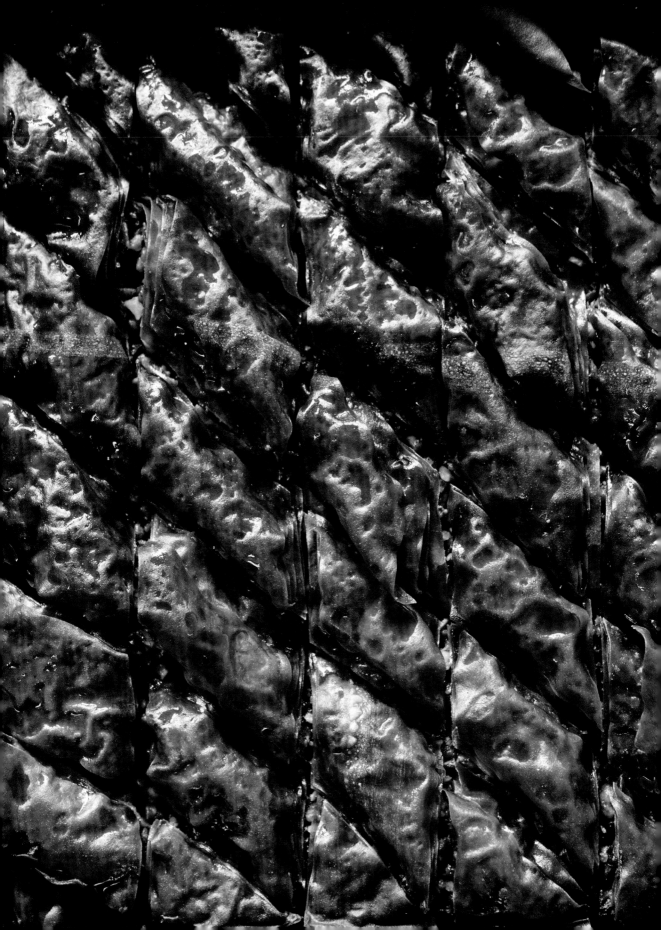

cranberries

Cranberries: native to North America and grown in acidic bogs – is it any wonder that they haven't seemed to curry much favour outside of their own turf? I call this the cranberry conundrum, because I am a big fan of these shiny, scarlet, tart, faintly bitter berries and I truly believe that they deserve your attention.

If we were to consider a spectrum of berries, cranberries would reside at one end and strawberries at the other. Both grow on vines and are red in colour, but that's where the similarities end. They are each other's opposite: cranberries must be cooked (as tempting as it may be to pop one in your mouth raw, please resist), whereas strawberries are best fresh (I will not hear otherwise). Cranberries are the berry of winter, strawbs the essence of summer. I love a strawberry as much as the next Brit – they are a total joy – but so are classy, jewel-like cranberries. These red berries have a lot to give – we just need to show them some care (and a little sweetness).

The season for cranberries runs from October to December and, outside of these months, you can't hunt them down for love nor money in the supermarkets, such is their temporary favour. The upside is that they freeze beautifully, which facilitates year-round consumption. I keep bags of them in the freezer and they can be used straight from frozen, no trimming or prep required.

Cranberries are the only berry found exclusively in North America. First discovered by the native Indians – for whom they were not just a food staple but also a symbol of peace and a form of medicine – today a whole industry exists around the cranberry in the states of Wisconsin and Massachusetts (who, together, produce more than 80% of the country's supply). While the domestic market is considerable, the agricultural cooperative Ocean Spray (set up in 1930) also sell into continental Europe, the United Kingdom and Mexico, and savvily offer products such as cranberry juice and 'craisins' (dried cranberries) year-round – after all, you can't have a Cosmopolitan without cranberry juice. Still, I believe fresh is where cranberries shine brightest: their very lack of sugar resulting in a more interesting flavour. As such, the recipes in this chapter tend to use cranberries in this raw form, although fresh and dried are often interchangeable depending not just on what you have to hand, but also whether your palate prefers sour and bitter or sweet tastes.

The importance of cranberries at the Christmas (or Thanksgiving) table cannot be underestimated. Not only do they stun visually, they also bring much-needed acidity and colour to the otherwise beige meal that is our (delicious!) Christmas lunch. It is that hit of sharpness from the cranberry sauce that saves you from falling into a rich-food-induced coma – it is my favourite thing on the table. Cranberry sauce is typically treated by the Christmas dinner cook in one of two ways: either relegated to a store-bought item (even though it could not be simpler or healthier to make your own), or made from scratch but over-embellished. Cranberries have so much complexity of flavour that adding cinnamon and ginger and red wine and cloves just results in something overworked and unpalatable. The best cranberry sauce is nothing but cranberries, water, sugar and a single bay leaf – trust me.

But cranberries are not just for Christmas: they are much more versatile than we give them credit for – and it's their bitterness that contributes to this flexibility. Cranberries are brilliant in baked goods (much like sour cherries) as their sharpness balances out the sweetness of ingredients such as white chocolate and pear (see the Cranberry and Pear Pie on page 150); they complement spice beautifully in both savoury and sweet situations; they are charming in chutneys, where they add nuance and piquancy; and they lend fabulous acidity to cocktails (see page 154).

As with most fruits and vegetables that are intense in colour and flavour, cranberries are very, very good for you: full of manganese and vitamins C and E. Like grapefruit, cranberries are anti-fungal – they can last for ages in the fridge – courtesy of the plant compound quercetin, which has also been linked to antioxidant, anti-inflammatory and anti-cancer properties: a true nutritional (and flavour!) powerhouse. (So, they're not *only* good for treating UTIs . . .)

saffron, yoghurt + cranberry persian(ish) rice

Serves 4–6

4.5 litres (1 gallon plus 3 cups) water

75g (3oz/generous ½ cup) Diamond kosher salt (don't panic)

400g (14oz/2 cups) basmati rice, rinsed thoroughly

2 good pinches of saffron

3 tbsp natural yoghurt

2 tsp boiling water

3 tbsp neutral oil

3 tbsp butter

60g (2½oz/heaped 1 cup) cranberries, fresh or frozen

10g (¼oz) each of coriander (cilantro), dill and flat-leaf parsley, finely chopped

equipment

25cm (10in) seasoned cast-iron or non-stick frying pan (skillet)

When I spent some time with my friend Bobak, learning more about Iranian food, he showed me how to make *tahdig* (a rice dish that features a delicious golden crust of rice, which forms at the bottom of the pan while cooking) and also introduced me to different types – ones layered with things like potatoes and even stale bread. He directed me, a *tahdig* novice, to start with Samin Nosrat's Persian-ish rice (from *Salt Fat Acid Heat*), where she makes the art of the *tahdig* feel accessible. This recipe is adapted from hers, with the addition of herbs and sharp cranberries to cut through the rich, buttery quality of the rice and saffron. This is delicious alongside stews (particularly Iranian ones), although I have been known to eat it by itself no problem.

1. Fill a large saucepan with the measured water and salt. Bring to the boil over a high heat, then add the rice and cook until al dente, around 6 minutes. Drain and immediately rinse under cold running water to stop it from cooking any further.

2. Meanwhile, crush the saffron in a pestle and mortar, then combine it with the yoghurt and boiling water until you have a gleaming golden-coloured mixture. Stir through a third of the cooked rice.

3. Set the frying pan over a medium heat, then add the oil and butter. When the butter has melted, add the yoghurt-rice mixture to the pan and level it out. Scatter the cranberries across the centre, followed by the herbs, then pile the remaining rice into the pan, mounding it gently in the middle (I've not yet found out why this shape is essential but every Iranian I've ever met tells you to do it this way). Using the handle of a wooden spoon, gently create 5–6 holes through to the bottom of the rice without disturbing the layers too much (these are to allow steam to escape as the rice cooks, which will enable the bottom to get crispy). Cook the rice for around 15 minutes until you see a golden crust beginning to form at the sides of the pan (you can use a spatula to gently have a little peek if you can't see anything from above). At this point, reduce the heat to low and cook for another 15 minutes, by which time the rice should be ready.

4. To unmould the rice, run a spatula around the edges of the pan to check the crust isn't sticking. Much as you would do for a tarte tatin, place a plate on top of the pan, then invert it in one swift movement. The rice should slip out in one piece. Serve.

charred savoy cabbage with cranberries + walnuts

Serves 2-3 as a main or 6-8 as a side

1 savoy cabbage, cut into 8 wedges
8 tbsp extra-virgin olive oil
2 tsp flaky sea salt
freshly ground black pepper
40g (1½oz/¼ cup) walnuts, toasted
30g (1oz/3½ tbsp) dried cranberries
2 tbsp white balsamic vinegar
(or standard balsamic)

for the tamari sauce
3 tbsp tamari (or soy sauce)
2 tsp fresh lime juice
1 tsp apple cider (or white wine)
vinegar
2 tbsp rapeseed (canola) oil (or other
neutral oil)
1 tbsp tahini
35g (1¼oz/4 tbsp) dried cranberries

equipment
blender

Cabbage is one of the humblest ingredients, yet the savoy cabbage has a regal elegance that other green veg can only dream of. Visually, it's a stunner, with its gorgeously round shape, striking green ombre and intricate veined leaves. Additionally, its robust texture ensures that it retains a degree of integrity where most other cruciferous vegetables fall apart under heat. Fittingly, it's the slowest-growing cabbage: good things come to those who wait.

Savoy cabbage is a very versatile vegetable – great for stuffing, super in slow-cooked soups and stews, and fabulous roasted, as here. I am indebted to Joshua McFadden, author of the brilliant *Six Seasons*, for this way of cooking cabbage. Paired with tamari, cranberries and walnuts, it's a punchy little number that also happens to be vegan.

1.   Preheat the oven to 220°C fan/240°C/475°F/gas 9. Line a large baking tray with baking paper.

2.   Spread the cabbage wedges out on the lined baking tray. Drizzle each wedge with a tablespoon of olive oil and season with the salt and pepper, ensuring all sides are covered. Roast in the oven for around 15 minutes, adding the walnuts and cranberries to the tray about 5 minutes before the end, to toast/warm through.

3.   Meanwhile, make the tamari sauce by adding all the ingredients to a blender and whizzing until smooth. The consistency should be a bit thicker than double (heavy) cream – add a teaspoon or two of water if you need to thin it out a bit.

4.   Remove the cabbage wedges from the oven when they are browned, crisped around the edges and slightly softened in the centre – don't be alarmed by extra-charred bits! Drizzle each wedge with a touch of white balsamic vinegar.

5.   To serve, spread a generous amount of the tamari sauce on a serving platter, arrange the roasted cabbage wedges on top and sprinkle with the toasted walnuts and cranberries.

cabbage + cranberry *thoran* pie

Serves 3-4

1 cabbage
2 carrots
1 tbsp ghee (or coconut oil)
1 tsp black mustard seeds
1 tsp cumin seeds, toasted
    and ground
¼ tsp ground turmeric
pinch of asafoetida
4–6 curry leaves, fresh (ideally)
    or dried
3 green chillies, pierced
1 tsp flaky sea salt
1 tsp sugar
juice of 1 lime
30g (1oz/½ cup) desiccated
    (unsweetened shredded)
    coconut, toasted
100g (3½oz/generous 1 cup) fresh
    (or frozen) cranberries
120g (4½oz) feta, crumbled

to assemble

6 filo (phyllo) pastry sheets
4 tbsp ghee (or coconut oil), melted
1 tsp nigella seeds (optional)

equipment

30cm (12in) pie dish or tin
    (I use a Falcon enamel large
    serving bowl)
food processor (useful, but
    not essential)
tea (dish) towel

I adore Keralan cabbage *thoran*, I adore Greek *spanakopita* and I adore the look of the French apple tart, *pastis gascon*, which is made with filo pastry. I wondered what would happen if I made a sort of Indian *spanakopita* and presented it like *pastis gascon*. And that's how this recipe came to be.

Indian cuisine often makes use of sour fruits in savoury cooking and, in this case, the cranberries cut through the richness of the ghee, the saltiness of the feta and the sweetness of the coconut. This makes a fabulous vegetarian dinner and can be easily made vegan by swapping the ghee for rapeseed (canola) oil and leaving out the cheese.

1. Preheat the oven to 170°C fan/190°C/375°F/gas 5. Place a baking sheet in the oven to heat up.

2. Finely slice/shred the cabbage and carrots – I use the slicing attachment of my food processor, but you could also do it by hand with a knife.

3. To make the filling, heat the ghee in a large frying pan (skillet) over a medium-high heat. Test that the ghee is at the right temperature by dropping a couple of mustard seeds into the pan – if they fizzle, it's hot enough. Add the rest of the mustard seeds. As soon as the mustard seeds start to pop, add the rest of the spices and the chillies. Add the cabbage and carrots, then stir-fry for around 5 minutes. Season with salt, sugar and lime juice, then stir in the coconut, fresh cranberries and feta. Set aside to cool.

4. To assemble the pie, cover the filo sheets with a slightly damp tea (dish) towel while you work, so that they don't dry out. Brush the pie dish with a thin layer of the melted ghee, then add a sheet of filo to the bottom of the tin. Brush this filo layer with more ghee, then place a second sheet of filo over the top. Repeat this process with 2 more layers of filo, leaving the edges overhanging the sides of the pie dish. Fill the pie dish with the cabbage *thoran* mixture, then fold the overhanging filo into the centre of the pie.

5. Separately, lay a sheet of filo on your work surface, brush with the ghee, scrunch it up, then arrange it on top of half of the pie. Repeat with another sheet of filo, placing this on the other half, creating a full pie 'lid'. Sprinkle with nigella seeds (if using). Place on the preheated baking sheet and bake for 20–25 minutes until the pastry is cooked through and golden brown.

pork + cranberry meatballs

Serves 4

150g (5oz) ricotta
1 small white onion, finely chopped
1 garlic clove, crushed
30g (1oz) flat-leaf parsley, finely
    chopped
20g (¾oz) dill, finely chopped
60g (2½oz) Parmesan, grated
80g (3oz/1⅛ cups) panko
    breadcrumbs (or regular
    breadcrumbs)
500g (1lb 2oz) minced (ground) pork
    (or beef), minimum 10% fat
1 egg
3 tsp fennel seeds, lightly toasted
2 tsp flaky sea salt
freshly ground black pepper
120g (4½oz/1¼ cups) fresh (or frozen)
    cranberries
vegetable oil, for cooking
15g (½oz) chives, finely chopped
    (I find scissors easiest for this),
    to garnish
zest of ½ lemon, to garnish

for the mustard cream sauce

1 tbsp butter
1 tbsp plain (all-purpose) flour
150ml (5fl oz/⅔ cup) chicken stock
2 tbsp crème fraîche
1 tbsp wholegrain mustard

TIP
Resting your meatballs is key
to ensuring they hold together,
have good flavour and a
moist texture. This also applies
to burgers.

Recently I was reminiscing about the IKEA Swedish meatballs: dense, round, savoury, all served with that creamy mustard-spiked sauce, chips and loganberry sauce – they were truly the highlight of our shopping trips when my brother and I were young. As soon as this memory crossed my mind, I knew I had to create a recipe in honour of them, and here it is! Serve with buttered cabbage and some form of crispy potato (wedges, roasties or chips). If you're not able to get hold of fresh or frozen cranberries then simply make the meatballs without the cranberries and serve them alongside a tart store-bought cranberry sauce.

1. Combine the ricotta, onion, garlic, parsley, dill, Parmesan and breadcrumbs in a large bowl and set aside for around 20 minutes so that the breadcrumbs can absorb the liquid and flavours.

2. Add the pork, egg, fennel seeds, salt and several grinds of black pepper, and mix it all together (it's easiest to use your hands for this). Roll the mixture into balls around 2cm (¾in) in diameter, incorporating a fresh cranberry into the centre of each one (think of them like mini cranberry Scotch eggs, with the cranberry replacing the egg). Once all the meatballs have been rolled out, place them on the lined baking tray and let them rest in the fridge for 1 hour (see Tip).

3. Preheat the oven to 160°C fan/180°C/350°F/gas 4. Line a baking tray with baking paper. (If roasting potatoes to serve alongside, cook these at a higher temperature before finishing off the meatballs.)

4. Heat a thin layer of oil in a large heavy-based pan over a medium-high heat. Brown the meatballs on all sides in batches, without over-crowding the pan. Once browned, return the meatballs to the baking tray and transfer to the oven for 10 minutes to finish cooking through.

5. Meanwhile, use the pan you fried the meatballs in to make your sauce (don't clean the pan – all those bits stuck to the bottom = flavour!). Reduce the heat to medium-low. You should be left with a decent amount of fat from the pork, but if this isn't the case add a tablespoon of butter and allow this to melt. Stir in the flour to create a paste and cook this out for a couple of minutes, then gradually whisk in the chicken stock until you have a smooth sauce. Stir in the crème fraîche and mustard.

6. To serve, spread the sauce on a platter, garnish with the chives and lemon zest, then pile on the meatballs.

cranberry brown butter bakewells

Makes 12

1 quantity of Sweet Almond Pastry
(see page 152)

for the cranberry coulis

250g (7oz/2½ cups) fresh (or frozen)
cranberries
80g (3oz/generous ⅓ cup) caster
(superfine) sugar
1½ tsp plain (all-purpose) flour
juice of 1 lemon
2 tbsp water
pinch of salt

for the frangipane

150g (5oz) butter, browned (take it as
far as you dare)
120g (4oz/generous ½ cup) caster
(superfine) sugar
finely grated zest of ½ orange
(optional)
2 tsp Disaronno (or ¼ tsp almond
essence)
3 eggs
120g (4oz/1¼ cups) ground almonds
15g (½oz/1 tbsp) plain (all-purpose)
flour
½ tsp fine sea salt
½ tsp baking powder

to assemble

50g (2oz/½ cup) fresh (or frozen and
defrosted) cranberries
10g (¼oz/2 tbsp) flaked (slivered)
almonds (optional)
icing (confectioners') sugar, for
dusting

equipment

12-hole cupcake/muffin tin
electric hand mixer (or stand mixer)
stick blender (or blender)

My grandfather loved a Bakewell and I am my grandfather's granddaughter. Throughout the year I make seasonal versions with different fruits, so you could call this my winter edition. Honestly, these are stunningly good. Making the frangipane with brown butter adds gorgeous toasty notes that feel appropriate for wintertime.

1. Roll the pastry into small balls then place one in each muffin hole. Press the pastry into the cavities, wetting the tips of your fingers to avoid getting too sticky with it, until all the muffin holes are lined with a roughly even layer of pastry. Place the muffin tray in the freezer for 1 hour.

2. Once the pastry is frozen, preheat the oven to 170°C fan/190°C/375°F/ gas 5.

3. Make the cranberry coulis by combining the ingredients in a small saucepan. Cook over a medium heat until soft and syrupy, then set aside to cool. When cool, blitz with a stick blender (I like to then pass the coulis through a sieve, but this is optional).

4. To make the brown butter frangipane, whisk together the browned butter, sugar, orange zest and Disaronno/almond essence. Add the eggs one at a time, whisking between each addition, then add the ground almonds. Sift in the flour, salt and baking powder, and mix until properly combined, but no longer!

5. Spoon a couple of teaspoons of the cranberry coulis into the base of the chilled pastry cases, then pipe or spoon the frangipane on top to fill. Push a couple of cranberries into each filled tart case, then sprinkle with the flaked almonds (if using). Bake for 15–20 minutes until the frangipane is golden brown and slightly puffed up. Place on a wire rack to cool completely.

6. Dust with icing sugar to serve.

TIP

When it comes to making pastry, cold temperatures and time are your best friends. If possible, make it the day before you want to use it, to give it plenty of time to hydrate.

cranberry + pear pie

Serves 6

1 lemon
6 Comice pears (about 650g/1lb 7oz)
45g (1¾oz/4 tbsp) cornflour
    (cornstarch)
100g (3½oz/½ cup) caster
    (superfine) sugar
340g (11½oz) fresh (or frozen)
    cranberries
½ tsp fine sea salt
1 quantity of Pie Dough
    (see page 231)
flour, for dusting
1 egg, beaten
2 tbsp demerara (turbinado) sugar
double (heavy) cream, to serve

equipment
20-22cm (8-9in) metal pie dish

TIP
A tip from Alison Roman: when it comes to baking anything with pie dough (flaky pastry), it always needs a lot longer in the oven than you think! See also the Blackcurrant, Blueberry and Liquorice Galette (page 222).

Confession time: in the past I've struggled to find any space in my heart for pears. Some appreciate their floral quality – I've even heard them described as herbaceous – but for me the lack of acidity is a problem. Basically, I'm an apple girl. That was until I pear-ed (sorry, not sorry) cranberries and pears in a pie and finally discovered what they were placed on this earth to do: balance out something a little sour/bitter. This is the best pie I've ever eaten. I can't even be modest about it.

The recipe for the pie dough can be found on page 231 and is best made the day before you want to make the pie.

1. Preheat the oven to 200°C fan/220°C/425°F/gas 7. Place a baking sheet in the oven to heat up.

2. Squeeze half of the lemon into a large bowl. Peel and core your pears, then cut them into rough chunks, about 2 x 1cm (¾ x ½in). Add these straight to the bowl as you go and toss them in the lemon juice to prevent them going brown.

3. In a separate bowl, whisk the juice from the other half of the lemon with the cornflour until it forms a smooth paste. Add this to the pears along with the caster sugar, cranberries and salt. Toss together.

4. Cut off a third of the pie dough and place it in the fridge to stay cold. On a lightly floured work surface (or piece of greaseproof paper), roll out the remaining dough to 3mm (⅛in) thick. Line your pie dish with this, making sure it's nicely nestled into the edges and leaving a 2–3cm (1in) overhang. Place in the fridge while you roll out the rest.

5. Remove the lined pie dish from the fridge and spoon in the filling, then place the pastry lid on top. Firmly press the pastry edges together to seal, then ease the overhanging pastry into the dish slightly, so that your filling is tucked in. Trim the overhanging pastry to around 2cm (¾in) all round, tuck the overhang underneath itself and, finally, crimp the edges. Chill the pie in the freezer for 15 minutes.

6. To bake, reduce the oven to 170°C fan/190°C/375°F/gas 5, brush the pastry with egg wash and sprinkle with the demerara sugar. Cut some vents in the top of the pie with a knife, then place on the preheated baking sheet. Bake for 1½ hours, turning halfway through, until deeply golden. If it's getting too dark, cover with foil. Leave to cool for 30 minutes minimum, ideally a full hour (*I know* – but it's the right thing to do). Serve with a generous pour of cold double cream.

sweet almond pastry

Makes enough for 10-12 Bakewell tarts (page 148)

130g (4½oz) unsalted butter
100g (3½oz/½ cup) caster
    (superfine) sugar
1 egg
2 drops almond extract
30g (1oz/⅓ cup) ground almonds
    (almond flour)
140g (4½oz/⅔ cup) plain
    (all-purpose) flour
heaped ¼ tsp baking powder
¼ tsp fine sea salt

equipment
food processor

I'll level with you: this pastry isn't the easiest to work with. However, it's got a lovely almond cakey-ness that works beautifully for the Cranberry Brown Butter Bakewells on page 148. Thankfully, all you'll be doing in that recipe is pushing the pastry into the case tins a bit like Play-Doh – child's play!

1. Put the butter and sugar in a food processor and blitz until smooth and fluffy. Add the egg and almond extract, then blitz until well combined. Add the ground almonds and blitz again, then sift in the remaining ingredients and pulse until the dough is homogenous.

2. Scoop the dough out with a spatula onto a piece of cling film (plastic wrap), then wrap and place in the fridge overnight to rest.

cranberry, orange + nutmeg breakfast muffins

Makes 9

There is great satisfaction in discovering or creating the 'ultimate' version of a dish, even if I have come to realise that you can't completely account for people's personal tastes. I'm not sure when I started getting obsessive about recipes, but I do remember spending a slightly frenzied week at university 'perfecting' the chocolate fondant at all costs. I am very fond of fellow food obsessives: writers such as Felicity Cloake ('How to make the perfect . . .' column in the *Guardian*), Kristen Miglore ('Genius Recipes' column on Food52) and, of course, Deb Perelman of the blog Smitten Kitchen. Deb has been getting manically obsessed with food since 2006 when she launched her wildly successful blog, and although she regularly pokes fun at her obsessive personality quirks, it is absolutely why we love her.

This recipe is perfection and is an adaptation of Deb's 'even more perfect blueberry muffins'. Primarily, I've tweaked the flavours: blueberry and lemon have become fresh cranberry and orange, plus a little nutmeg. To make the muffins more breakfast appropriate I have settled on Greek yoghurt and reduced the sugar. I have also discovered how wonderful white spelt flour is in muffins, giving them a lovely softness (if less height).

This is a one-bowl affair and the work of mere minutes, especially if you've got ready-made muffin cases. Thank you, Deb, for your obsessiveness.

1. Preheat the oven to 170°C fan/190°C/375°F/gas 5. Line the muffin tin with 9 muffin cases.

2. In a large bowl, whisk together the melted butter, yoghurt, egg, caster sugar and orange zest.

3. In a small bowl or cup, whisk together the baking powder, bicarbonate of soda, nutmeg and salt. Add this to the melted butter mix and combine thoroughly. Fold in the flour and then the cranberries. You will think that the batter is too thick and that there are too many cranberries, but everything is as it's supposed to be.

4. Divide the mixture among the 9 muffin cases, then sprinkle each muffin with a teaspoon of demerara sugar (it sounds like a lot, but this textural contrast is part of what makes these muffins shine, so don't skimp on this). Bake for 25–35 minutes until the tops are golden and a skewer inserted into the middles comes out clean.

70g (3oz) butter, melted and left to cool slightly
150g (5oz/scant ⅔ cup) Greek yoghurt (or soured cream)
1 egg
90g (3¼oz/scant ½ cup) caster (superfine) sugar
zest of 1 orange
1½ tsp baking powder
¼ tsp bicarbonate of soda (baking soda)
¾ tsp ground nutmeg
¼ tsp fine sea salt
195g (7oz/1½ cups) white spelt (or plain/all-purpose) flour
180g (6oz/scant 2 cups) fresh (or frozen) cranberries
9 tsp (about 40g/1½oz) demerara (turbinado) sugar

equipment
12-hole muffin tin
muffin cases

ALTERNATIVES
If you don't have cranberries to hand, you could sub them for Deb's original blueberries or another tart round berry, such as blackcurrants. For blueberries, swap the orange zest for lemon zest and the nutmeg for ground coriander (yes, really). For blackcurrants, use lemon zest and mixed spice.

the *and just like that . . .* cosmo

Cranberry Vodka • Makes 500ml (17fl oz/scant 2 cups)

250g (9oz/2½ cups) cranberries, each
   cut in half
500ml (17fl oz/scant 2 cups) vodka
150g (5oz/¾ cup) granulated sugar

equipment
1-litre (1-quart) glass jar or bottle

This is the very best way to consume cranberries year-round. Serve with lime and soda water or use in the updated Cosmo recipe below.

1. Combine the ingredients in the sealable jar. Leave in a cool, dark place for 1 week, stirring (or swirling) every couple of days. You can start using it from this point, but it will only get better after a few additional weeks of steeping.

The *And Just Like That . . .* Cosmo • Makes 2 cocktails

100ml (3½fl oz/scant ½ cup) cranberry
   vodka (see above)
40ml (1½fl oz/2 tbsp plus 2 tsp)
   grapefruit syrup (see below)
20ml (¾fl oz/4 tsp) fresh lime juice
20ml (¾fl oz/4 tsp) dry white vermouth
ice, for shaking
strip or twist of orange zest, to garnish

for the grapefruit syrup
2 strips of grapefruit zest
100g (3½oz/½ cup) caster (superfine)
   sugar
100ml (3½fl oz/scant ½ cup) water
1 bay leaf

equipment
cocktail shaker (or large jar)
cocktail strainer or small sieve (fine
   mesh strainer)
2 chilled cocktail glasses

In recent years, we've been forced to spend a bit more time indoors, so I've started to get more familiar with shaking up my own cocktails. I kept reminiscing about that *Sex and the City*-era classic, the Cosmopolitan, and made one according to the classic recipe. Sadly, it wasn't as fabulous as I had remembered: the acidity was high and the balance felt off. I had hoped that it would transport me to some cool bar in New York City and allow me to imagine myself as Carrie Bradshaw for a few moments (was anyone else indulging in these sorts of escapist fantasies while we were all trapped at home?). It didn't. And so, in honour of *And Just Like That . . .* (if you know, you know), here is the Cosmo revival.

1. To make the grapefruit syrup, combine the ingredients in a small saucepan and set over a high heat. Bring to the boil and allow to bubble for a minute or two, then remove from the heat and leave to cool. Remove the grapefruit zest and bay leaf.

2. To make the cocktail, fill a cocktail shaker with ice and add the vodka, syrup, lime juice and vermouth. Place the lid on firmly and shake vigorously until the cocktail shaker feels ice cold. Strain into chilled martini glasses and garnish with the orange zest.

tea

The power of tea to soothe and restore goes back to its birthplace, China, and their legend of the 'divine farmer' Shen Nong, who consumed seventy-two poisons but was revived by a single tea leaf when it drifted into his mouth. Today, tea is the second most-consumed drink on the planet (after water), which says a lot about its universal pull.

When the Dutch brought tea back to Europe in the seventeenth century, it quickly became popular with the English aristocracy and, as Great Britain expanded its colonial power, so interest in tea spread around the world. The British and tea go way back – unfortunately not always in a way that reflects well on the Brits (a familiar story). It's the ultimate irony, of course, that something that led to the First Opium War in the nineteenth century should come to represent comfort and reconciliation today. In anticipation of trouble brewing – or indeed, once it has already brewed – asking your adversary whether they'd like a cup of tea is the ultimate shorthand for 'I'm sorry, let's be friends again'. It's comparable to a comforting hug from a loved one at the end of a tough day.

One of the biggest exporters of tea in the world is Sri Lanka. And, as I discovered on a recent trip there, the tea country in the central region is magical: uncompromisingly hilly, lushly verdant and perpetually misty. I doubt there are many nicer-smelling places in the world: the scent of tea fills the air, accompanied by a grassy, basil-like aroma. Heady, but in a gentle way. Ceylon (i.e. Sri Lankan) tea is world-renowned, but before it becomes the coveted silver tip tea that we brew in our cups, it goes through a lengthy, diligent process of picking, drying, rolling and sorting.

At Kinellan Tea Factory in Ella, tea leaves are picked by female workers and carried in woven sacks on their heads to the factory. Once weighed, the leaves are laid out in long, wide trays, which send air in and around them to start the drying process. After being semi-dried, the leaves are sent down through a trapdoor in the floor, falling directly into huge, laterally rotating machines. The effect of these is quite something: bullying, dominating, overbearing. Manufactured in the 1960s, 70s and 80s, they are relics of Sri Lanka's British occupation and reference a dystopian industrial age. Surprisingly, the purpose of these juggernauts is to very gently roll the tea leaves before they are placed on open shelves to ferment. Once this process is complete, the leaves are dried in the hottest, most airless chamber you can imagine, followed by careful grading, sieving and sorting. Eventually, large bags are filled with 20kg of tea, ready to be priced by tea brokers and subsequently sent off to the tea auctions in Colombo.

Different teas go to different markets: the lightest to Europe, the strongest to Britain. Sri Lankans also enjoy a stronger brew – although they tend to swerve the addition of milk. I suspect this is down to the sugariness of their sweets, which demand a tea of sufficient strength and bitterness to balance them out, but it could also be down to what they're used to: in the Sri Lankan tea plantations of old, workers would smuggle tea leaves home and complete the processing of the tea in their backyards. This was done with household tools such as the *wangediya saha molgassa* (a large pestle and mortar, which stands on the floor), and this rough treatment of the tea leaves resulted in a stronger, more bitter brew.

There are almost as many ways of preparing tea as there are cultures on our planet. And there are many different types of tea, too. If you go into the tea mecca that is Fortnum & Mason on Piccadilly in London, it is likely you will be told that no tea should taste bitter if it's prepared properly. But the typical tea experience is not one in which you're heating your water to *exactly* the temperature specified for individual teas (around 90–95°C/194–203°F for black, 80°C/176°F for white), and brewing for *exactly* the specified number of minutes, nor are you necessarily only ever drinking the very finest tea leaves in the land. The method of preparation will significantly affect how much bitterness is extracted from tea, along with several other factors: the age of the leaves, the cut of the leaves (in the case of tea bags) and the variety. For example, lapsang souchong involves the cultivation of older leaves to give that smoky, intense flavour, while the leaves for Irish tea are cut in a way that deliberately leads to a stouter, more bitter brew. In my view, you wouldn't drink the latter without milk, which brings us right back to that concept of soothing bitterness with dairy (see pages 16–17).

In this chapter, I explore the bitterness – and sometimes smokiness – present in a few different types of tea: lapsang souchong, British breakfast tea, South African rooibos, Japanese sencha tea leaves and powdery green matcha, as well as Indian masala chai with its bitter notes of cardamom. All different, all wonderful, and all soothing for the soul.

tomato + lapsang souchong salad

Serves 2-4

2 large tomatoes, e.g. bull's heart or beef (about 700g/1lb 9oz total weight)
1½ tsp flaky sea salt
4 tbsp high-quality extra-virgin olive oil
1 tbsp lapsang souchong tea
1½ tsp sherry vinegar
handful of basil leaves
focaccia or ciabatta, to serve

equipment
pestle and mortar or spice blender

Tea and tomatoes have aroma compounds in common, so there's something surprisingly harmonious about this combination. The black of the tea also looks striking over the bright red tomatoes. You could add torn mozzarella to this to make it a bit more substantial.

1.   Cut the tomatoes into rough chunks and put in a bowl along with the salt and olive oil. Leave to marinate for 5 minutes.

2.   Meanwhile, crush the lapsang souchong to a fine powder using a pestle and mortar or spice blender.

3.   To serve, add the vinegar to the tomatoes, toss, then transfer to a platter (juices and all). Liberally sprinkle the ground lapsang souchong over the tomatoes, then garnish with basil leaves. This is lovely served with focaccia or ciabatta to drag through the leftover tomato juices on the plate.

tempura french beans with lapsang souchong dipping sauce

Serves 4 as a snack

200g (7oz) French beans, trimmed at
    stem end
vegetable oil, for deep-frying

for the tempura
75g (3oz/scant ⅔ cup) cornflour
    (cornstarch)
65g (2½oz/½ cup) plain (all-purpose)
    flour
¼ tsp fine sea salt
1 egg, fridge-cold
120ml (4fl oz/½ cup) soda water,
    fridge-cold
50ml (2fl oz/3 tbsp plus 1 tsp) vodka
    (or replace with additional soda
    water), fridge-cold

for the dipping sauce
1 tbsp lapsang souchong tea leaves
2 tbsp hot water
2 tbsp rice vinegar
2 tbsp soy sauce
½ spring onion (scallion), finely sliced
¼ tsp finely grated fresh root ginger
2 tsp sesame oil
¼ tsp dried chilli (hot pepper) flakes
    (or more, if you like it hot)
    or chilli oil, to taste

equipment
a deep-fat fryer or a temperature
    probe are useful, but
    not essential

These long thin green beans look picture-perfect fried in tempura batter. They're served alongside a dipping sauce where the addition of lapsang souchong adds a resolute smokiness and slight bitterness, which is what makes these so moreish.

My go-to recipe for tempura is adapted from the one and only J. Kenji López-Alt and the use of vodka here, although optional, helps to inhibit gluten formation so that the batter lasts a bit longer than it usually would. The ingredients for the tempura batter must be really cold – make sure to store everything in the fridge ahead of making. Finally, feel free to play around with this recipe – squid, prawns (shrimp) or oyster mushrooms would all work well here.

1. Start by making the dipping sauce. Add the tea leaves to the hot water and leave to steep for 5 minutes. Strain out the leaves, then stir in the rest of the ingredients. Set aside.

2. In a heavy-based pan or deep-fat fryer, heat the oil to 170°C (338°F), ready to fry the French beans.

3. To make the tempura batter, whisk together the dry ingredients in a bowl. In a separate bowl or jug, whisk together the wet ingredients. Add the wet ingredients to the dry and use chopsticks or a knife to roughly mix everything together until just combined – you want there to still be pockets of flour, rather than a homogenous batter.

4. Dip the green beans into the batter one at a time and then transfer to the fryer. Cook for around 3 minutes, then remove with a slotted spoon to drain on kitchen paper. Work in batches, if needed.

5. Serve immediately alongside the dipping sauce.

TIP
Vodka is a surprisingly useful ingredient: it inhibits gluten formation in batters and doughs where you want to preserve lightness or flakiness; it inhibits crystallisation in ice creams (helpful for the no-churn variety); and it is also a flavour carrier (hence why *penne alla vodka* is so well-loved).

mushrooms on toast with sencha butter

Serves 2

50g (2oz) softened butter, plus extra
    for greasing
leaves from 1 green tea bag
    (around 2 tsp)
½ garlic clove, grated
small handful of coriander (cilantro)
    leaves, very finely chopped
½ tsp maple syrup
4 portobello mushrooms
1 tbsp olive oil
¼ tsp fine sea salt
freshly ground black pepper
2 slices of sourdough
squeeze of lemon juice, if liked

This is a subtle, bitter twist on a well-loved classic that is perfect for breakfast or a light lunch.

1. Preheat the oven to 170°C fan/190°C/375°F/gas 5.

2. Mix together the softened butter, tea leaves, garlic, coriander and maple syrup to create a flavoured butter.

3. Butter an oven dish that can hold the mushrooms snugly in a single layer. Add the mushrooms, then divide the flavoured butter among them, adding roughly a teaspoonful on top of each. Drizzle over the olive oil, season the mushrooms generously, then bake for 20–25 minutes until they are tender and surrounded by buttery juices.

4. Toast the bread, then top each slice with a couple of mushrooms and pour over any juices left in the dish. Add a squeeze of lemon, if liked.

matcha basque cheesecake

Serves 8-10

2 x 340g (12oz) packs full-fat cream
    cheese

225g (8oz/1 cup plus 2 tbsp) caster
    (superfine) sugar

1½ tsp flaky sea salt

5 eggs

150ml (5fl oz/⅔ cup) soured cream

150ml (5fl oz/⅔ cup) double (heavy)
    cream

30g (1oz/¼ cup) plain (all-purpose)
    flour (gluten-free flour also works
    here)

2 tbsp high-quality matcha powder

equipment
20cm (8in) springform baking tin

Here's an unpopular opinion: I've never been keen on the biscuit base in a cheesecake. Hence why the Basque cheesecake – which has none – is for me the best possible version of this dessert (and all the quicker to make, too). You cook this cheesecake at a high temperature so that the top burns, and this adds a bitter note that offers both visual and flavour contrast to the dense, creamy baked cheesecake underneath. If you like Jewish or Polish-style cheesecakes, then this will be your bag. All credit to Nicola Lamb for introducing me to this one.

This must be made the day before you want to eat it and left overnight in the fridge to set and chill (in fact, it peaks on day three): it's the secret to the cheesecake's dense creaminess. If you don't give it time to relaxxx, then you'll find the texture a bit more like a frittata . . . not what we're after here. This is gorgeous served with fresh cherries or strawberries.

I buy premium-grade matcha tea from Clearspring or Sous Chef.

1. Preheat the oven to 240°C fan/260°C/500°F/gas 9 (essentially, the highest your oven can go). Line the baking tin with baking paper (not in the way you would line a Christmas cake, rather just one big piece of paper pushed into the tin – it's supposed to look rustic!).

2. Place the cream cheese in a bowl and whisk to loosen it up and get rid of any lumps – try to avoid adding air into the mixture (we're going for a dense, thick mix here). Beat in the sugar and salt until melted into the mixture, then beat in the eggs, one by one.

3. In a separate bowl, whisk together the soured cream and double cream. Combine the flour and matcha powder, then sift this over the sour cream mixture and whisk to incorporate. Fold this into the cream cheese.

4. Pour the mixture into your baking tin and tap it 3–4 times on the work surface to get rid of any lingering air bubbles. Place the cheesecake in the oven and turn the temperature down to 210°C fan/230°C/450°F/gas 8. Bake for 40–45 minutes. If you find that the top isn't getting dark enough, then turn the oven back up to the original temperature for the last 5 minutes. The cheesecake should still be wobbly in the middle (it will firm up significantly as it cools). Allow to cool and then place in the fridge to set for at least 6 hours (ideally overnight).

TIP

It's not just this cheesecake that deserves an overnight rest in the fridge – every cheesecake benefits from this, tempting though it is to eat them immediately (see also the Coffee and Biscoff No-Bake Cheesecake on page 188).

strawberry, bitter lemon + rooibos sorbet

Makes around 1 litre (1¾ pints/4 cups)

3 lemons: 2 topped and tailed
    (minimally); 1 juiced
400g (14oz/2 cups) granulated (or
    caster/superfine) sugar
800g (1lb 12oz) strawberries, hulled
2 rooibos tea bags

equipment
food processor
ice cream machine (ideally)

This is inspired by the infamous River Café strawberry sorbet; however, I have increased the lemon, reduced the sugar and added rooibos tea, which blends seamlessly. Somehow, the bitterness of the lemon and the tea brings out the sweetness and flavour of the strawberries – like magic!

1. Cut the topped-and-tailed lemons in half lengthways, then into quarters, then cut each quarter into 4 pieces. In a food processor, blitz together the lemon pieces and sugar until a damp paste is formed (it doesn't have to be perfectly smooth). Add the strawberries, lemon juice and the contents of the rooibos tea bags and blitz until smooth. Transfer to the fridge and chill for 1–2 hours.

2. Strain the mixture into a bowl through a sieve (fine mesh strainer), adding back a couple of tablespoons of the pulp for a bit of texture. Churn in an ice cream machine, according to the manufacturer's instructions. Alternatively, place in an airtight container in the freezer and whisk after 30–45 minutes to break up the ice crystals. Repeat 3–4 times until you have a smooth mixture, then allow to freeze fully.

TIP
If churning this by hand, add 1 tbsp vodka to the mix to inhibit the crystallisation – this should result in a smoother sorbet.

builder's tea + digestives ice cream

Makes around 1 litre (1¾ pints/4 cups)

335ml (11fl oz/generous 1⅓ cups)
double (heavy) cream
270ml (9fl oz/1 cup plus 2 tbsp) whole
milk
100g (3½oz/½ cup) caster (superfine)
sugar
2 breakfast tea bags (I like Irish
breakfast tea because it's
quite strong)
¼ tsp fine sea salt
6 egg yolks
7 digestive biscuits,
very coarsely crushed

equipment

ice cream machine
freezer-proof container

Is there anything more British than a cup of builder's tea and a digestive biscuit? I'll wait.

1. Combine the cream, milk, half of the sugar, the tea from the tea bags and salt in a medium saucepan and heat until steaming (but not simmering!). Turn the heat off and allow the mixture to steep for 1 hour.

2. Once the milk and cream mixture has had its steeping time, heat it back up to steaming. Separately, combine the egg yolks and the remaining sugar in a bowl and whisk together for a couple of minutes until pale and fluffy. Pour half of the steaming milk mixture into the egg yolks, whisking as you go. Now place the saucepan with the remaining milk mixture back on the heat and add the egg yolk mixture to the pan, whisking to ensure everything is fully combined. Cook the custard over a medium heat, stirring continuously with a whisk until it starts to thicken. It's ready when the custard coats the back of a spoon and a clear path is left when you drag your finger through it.

3. Pass the custard through a fine sieve, then cover the surface with cling film (plastic wrap) and allow it to cool. Once cool, chill the custard down for at least a couple of hours, but ideally overnight.

4. Churn the custard in an ice cream machine, according to the manufacturer's instructions, then stir through the crushed digestives. Freshly churned, the ice cream will have a soft-serve texture that I really love, but if you want it to be firmer, place it in a container in the freezer for around 4 hours to fully set.

NOTE

British digestive biscuits can be found in the international aisle of larger supermarkets or ordered from online retailers. They're a semi-sweet biscuit with a malted flavour and coarse, sandy texture.

TIP

Adding half of the sugar to the milk helps to stop it catching – this is a good method to use when making any form of custard.

cardamom chai shortbread

Makes 12 biscuits (cookies)

Cardamom is one of my favourite spices because it brings a myriad of qualities to the table: floral, bracing, woody, astringent, bitter. The word comes from an Arabic root meaning 'to warm' and somehow, despite some of its more challenging qualities, it ultimately does just that: wrap you in a delicate yet intoxicating hug. These biscuits, classic Scottish shortbread crossed with Indian chai tea, were inspired by a specific moment on a trip I took to Sri Lanka: at the Galle Face protest site we were offered steaming cups of chai, heady with cardamom and spicy with black pepper. It was a magical, comforting moment and one that brought everyone together. These biscuits have the power to bring people together, too.

1. Beat together the butter, sugar, spices and tea leaves until pale and fluffy – this will take 4–5 minutes with an electric mixer. Add the flour and salt and mix on a low speed until just combined, no longer.

2. Tip the dough out onto a sheet of cling film (plastic wrap) and shape it into a thick log. Wrap up in the cling film, then chill overnight (or for at least 2 hours).

3. Preheat the oven to 160°C fan/180°C/350°F/gas 4 and line two large baking trays with a silicone mat or greaseproof paper (if you don't have two baking trays, you can simply cook the biscuits in two batches).

4. To make the tea sugar coating, combine the granulated sugar and tea in a wide, shallow dish. Unwrap the dough log, use a pastry brush to coat it in the egg white, then roll the log in the tea sugar until evenly coated.

5. Cut the dough log into 12 rounds and place on the baking trays, well spaced. Bake for 15–20 minutes until the edges are firm and starting to turn golden but the middles still look light. Remove from the oven and leave to cool completely before indulging.

200g (7oz) butter, softened
90g (3¼oz/scant ½ cup) caster (superfine) sugar
1 tsp ground ginger
1 tsp ground cinnamon
¼ tsp freshly ground black pepper
¼ tsp freshly ground cardamom
leaves from 1 black tea bag
300g (10½oz/scant 2½ cups) plain (all-purpose) flour
½ tsp fine sea salt

for the tea sugar coating
50g (2oz/¼ cup) granulated sugar
leaves from 2 black tea bags (e.g. breakfast tea, earl grey, assam, etc.)
1 egg white, lightly whisked

equipment
electric hand mixer (optional)

TIP

I'm probably sounding like a broken record at this point, but – truly – any biscuit or cookie dough, as well as pastry, hugely benefits from an overnight rest in the fridge. It ensures that the flour is properly hydrated and that the gluten has had a chance to relax. What this means for you is dough that is easier to work with and a better result when baked.

coffee

Without coffee Europeans might have continued to spend a considerable proportion of their lives mildly drunk, as had been the case since the Middle Ages. I talked earlier about the beer-drinking culture that developed in the West (page 98) and why, as a way of making water safe to drink, it was key to our survival. But while consuming alcohol might have kept us alive, it didn't exactly help us to excel. As Michael Pollan identifies in his book *This Is Your Mind on Plants*, it wasn't until caffeine arrived on the scene, in the form of coffee, tea and hot cocoa, that human productivity started to climb.

The coffee tree, like *Homo sapiens*, originated in East Africa. Legend states that, in the ninth century, a young Ethiopian goat herder first tried the bright red fruit of the coffee plant after he saw his goats get a buzz from consuming them. But the cultivation of coffee seems truly to have begun in Yemen in the fourteenth century, where the plant was given the Arabic name *qahwa*, and the process of roasting and grinding coffee beans started. This coffee was bitter, grittier stuff than what we're used to today, yet there must have been a sense that it was special because the Yemenis attempted to limit its spread by only selling on infertile coffee beans. Such efforts were ultimately rendered pointless as fertile seeds were smuggled into south India at the beginning of the seventeenth century, subsequently adopted by Dutch and French colonists and eventually taken to Latin America, setting Brazil up for its current status as the largest producer of coffee in the world.

Today, coffee is not only one of the most popular drinks, it's also one of the most fashionable. Where tea is comforting, coffee is cool: it represents action, focus, productivity. The branded cup that you carry into work each morning says something about you (and acts as a walking advertisement for whichever coffee company you decided to buy from that day); tea brands can only dream of having this sort of social currency.

Coffee is one of the easier sells in this book, in spite of just how bitter it can be, because most people's introduction to the drink comes by way of a milky (and often sweetened) latte or cappuccino, which eases us into coffee's bitter qualities. Even through the milkiness of a latte it's possible to detect the nutty, malty, toasty flavours of coffee, although it's true that to venture into the land of espressos or black coffee is to realise that it can also be fragrant, powerful, tart, zingy, rich, tannic, edgy.

The process of producing coffee beans in many ways echoes that of chocolate (see page 194): the beans are separated from the fruit ('coffee cherries'), then fermented, dried and roasted. Un-roasted green coffee beans are highly acidic and extremely tart, but the roasting process lessens these properties and introduces some bitterness to balance them out. Too little roasting and acidity dominates; too much and you lose many of the acids and tannins that give coffee its complexity and body: it's all about finding that bitter balance.

But while chocolate is typically delivered to us in ready-wrapped bars, with coffee there is further ceremony. Part of coffee's magic and mystique lies in the expertise and gadgets required to go from bean to cup: boiling, manual filtration, machine filtration, percolation, the French press and the espresso machine are all options, each offering different levels of extraction, which translates to different strengths and flavour profiles. In short, the way in which coffee is transformed into a cup of joe matters. And this process is not only a perfect illustration of how flavour can be balanced, it also yields one of the most complex flavours in the world, with more than 800 aroma components contributing earthy, floral, buttery, toasty, smoky, spicy, gamey notes. No wonder milk and cream are often employed to round them out.

The making of coffee naturally brings us to the ubiquitous coffee shop. Coffee houses first appeared in the Islamic world of the sixteenth century and quickly became hubs for free speech and community organising – so much so that in 1511, the governor of Mecca closed all the city's coffee houses. Fast-forward to 1650s London and coffee houses started cropping up with speed, offering a non-boozy alternative to taverns (which were often places of conflict and violence). Coffee houses became spots for intellectual engagement, progress and revolution. Whatever fields you dabbled in, there was a coffee house for that: literature, stocks, science, etc. These were 'penny universities': in Pollan's words, 'you paid a penny for the coffee but the information was free', and it was powerful stuff. The French Revolution started in a coffee house. As did the London Stock Exchange, Lloyd's of London and publications such as the *Spectator*. Though no longer hubs of revolution, coffee shops today remain a form of social altar: city workers congregate during their breaks; friends meet; individuals set themselves up to work; others pass through. They're a constant hive of activity.

Beyond the hot drinks that fuel us daily, coffee is an ingredient that can be used in your cooking. It brings a powerful combination of bitter, sour (acidic) and umami flavour, which in savoury dishes adds depth, and in sweet applications excites all of your taste buds at the same time – it's very much grounds for culinary brilliance.

mushroom + three cheese quesadillas

Makes 6 small quesadillas

25g (1oz) butter
250g (9oz) mixed mushrooms
75g (3oz) Parmesan, grated
6 small (18cm/7in) tortillas
50g (2oz) feta, crumbled into
    small pieces
200g (7oz) mozzarella, torn into
    small pieces

for the coffee spice mix
½ tsp cumin seeds
½ tsp espresso powder
1 tsp dried oregano
½ tsp chipotle chilli powder
    (or cayenne pepper)
½ tsp ground cinnamon

equipment
pestle and mortar (or spice grinder)

Quesadillas – the Latin version of a cheese toastie – promise so much and yet frequently disappoint. I'm convinced this is because we expect melted cheese to carry the whole thing when it simply doesn't. Where a cheese toastie typically contains a decent amount of strong, umami-rich cheese, such as Cheddar, quesadillas are more likely to use mild cheeses like mozzarella. And where a cheese toastie offers the robust presence and flavour of bread, the tortillas used for quesadillas are nothing but a paper-thin vessel. This is why the filling is critical – and that's where these quesadillas triumph: mixed mushrooms offer umami flavour and texture; the addition of feta and Parmesan to the cheese mix adds essential saltiness; and the Mexican-inspired coffee spice mix that you sprinkle over the filling wakes up your palate.

1. Start by making the spice mix. In a small dry frying pan (skillet), lightly toast the cumin seeds until fragrant, then lightly crush in a pestle and mortar (or spice grinder). Stir through the rest of the spices and set aside.

2. Heat the butter in a large non-stick frying pan over a high heat, add the mushrooms and fry until golden brown. Tip onto a plate lined with kitchen paper and set aside.

3. Thoroughly wipe out the pan using a piece of kitchen paper, ready to cook the quesadillas. Before cooking, make sure you have all the ingredients prepped and ready to go. I find it easiest to make up 6 individual piles of cheese (made up of a little of the feta and mozzarella).

4. Reheat the pan over a medium heat. When hot, sprinkle half a tablespoon of grated Parmesan over half of the pan and let it melt (err on the side of cooking the quesadillas low'n'slow). Once melted, place a tortilla on top of the cheese so that half of the tortilla has cheese underneath it. Add a thin layer of the cooked mushrooms, followed by a generous pinch or two of the spice mix, followed by the mixed cheeses, then fold over the half of the tortilla that is not adhered to the Parmesan. Let the quesadilla cook until the Parmesan has turned golden, then use a spatula to flip it over. Cook until the other side has turned lightly golden and the cheese inside has melted.

5. Remove to a plate, then repeat to make the rest. These are best eaten straight out of the pan, or you can keep them warm in a low oven while you cook them all.

pork with tomatoes + chipotle espresso butter

Serves 2

375ml (12fl oz/1½ cups) water
1 tbsp flaky sea salt
300g (10½oz) pork loin
2 tbsp olive oil

for the tomato sauce
2 tbsp olive oil
1 small onion, finely sliced
½ tsp flaky sea salt, or more to taste
1 garlic clove, crushed
1 bay leaf
¼ tsp smoked hot paprika
½ long red chilli (optional)
400g (14oz) cherry tomatoes
freshly ground black pepper

for the chipotle espresso butter
20g (¾oz) butter
¼ tsp chipotle chilli powder (or a pinch of cayenne pepper)
½ tsp ground coffee
½ tsp maple syrup
½ tsp tamari (or soy sauce)
½ tsp sherry vinegar

TIP

For cuts of meat like pork tenderloin and chicken breast, which can lean towards being bland and dry, brining is a game-changing technique. It ensures juicy meat that is seasoned all the way through – and it couldn't be simpler.

This is an easy dinner for two, made up of simple, classic flavours, but it is the subtle bitterness and spiciness of the chipotle espresso butter that provides a little additional excitement for the taste buds.

1. Combine the water and salt in a bowl large enough to hold the pork tenderloin curled in the bottom. Add the pork and set aside.

2. For the tomatoes, heat the olive oil in a heavy-based pan over a low heat. Add the sliced onion and salt, and sweat down for around 10 minutes – you don't want this to get any colour. Add the garlic, bay leaf, paprika and red chilli (if using) and increase the heat to medium-low. Add the tomatoes and cook for 10–15 minutes until the tomatoes have softened (and some have burst). Season to taste with salt and black pepper and leave on the lowest heat to keep warm.

3. Set a seasoned cast-iron pan (or non-stick frying pan/skillet) over a high heat. Open the windows and turn on the extractor fan.

4. Remove the pork from the brine and thoroughly dry with kitchen paper. Add the olive oil to the hot pan, wait for 30 seconds for the oil to heat up and then add the pork loin. Cook on the first side for 2½ minutes, during which time it should have developed a golden crust (if it hasn't, turn the heat up further). Cook for 1½ minutes on each of the other 3 sides in turn (this will result in a perfectly pink middle, but if you want it cooked a little more then cook for 2–2½ minutes per side). Remove the pork loin from the pan, wrap in foil and leave to rest for 8 minutes.

5. Meanwhile, make the chipotle espresso butter. Melt the butter in a pan, then remove from the heat, add the rest of the ingredients and stir together until well combined.

6. To serve, spoon the tomato sauce onto a serving platter, slice the pork tenderloin and arrange over the tomatoes, then pour over the chipotle espresso butter.

ancho coffee short ribs

Serves 6

2kg (4lb 8oz) bone-in short ribs,
    prepped
Diamond kosher salt, for seasoning
    the short ribs
1½ tbsp coriander seeds
1½ tbsp cumin seeds
1½ tbsp fennel seeds
1½ tbsp dried oregano
1½ tbsp ground coffee
2 tbsp vegetable oil
6 banana shallots (around 400g/1lb),
    peeled
½ tbsp chipotle chilli powder
4 bay leaves
6 garlic cloves, thinly sliced
1 tbsp finely grated fresh root ginger
1 cinnamon stick
1 dried ancho chilli, split in half
2 tbsp tomato paste
1 x 330ml (11fl oz) bottle of Corona
    beer
500ml (18fl oz/2 cups) chicken or
    beef stock
2 tbsp soy sauce
1 tbsp white balsamic vinegar

for the quick-pickled onions
2 red onions, thinly sliced
juice of 6 limes
pinch of fine sea salt

for the fresh corn polenta
10 ears of corn
50g (2oz) butter
½ tsp fine sea salt
freshly ground black pepper
50g (2oz) feta, finely crumbled
    (optional)

equipment
large casserole dish (Dutch oven)
pestle and mortar (or spice grinder)
stick blender or food processor

Short ribs are a real crowd-pleaser and here we have flavours inspired by Mexican *mole*, as well as the bitter depths of coffee and beer. I serve this with a fresh corn polenta, which is simple but admittedly requires you to remove the kernels from 10 ears of corn . . . it's worth it for an accompaniment that is gently sweet, rich and yet fresh. But if you can't be bothered, or corn is out of season, then soft polenta would do in a heartbeat (see the recipe on page 126). Or you could shred the short ribs and use them in tacos. A green salad is nice with this, too.

If possible, do season the short ribs the night before.

1.   Season the ribs with kosher salt, then put in a couple of large sealable plastic bags and place in the fridge for at least a couple of hours, but ideally overnight.

2.   When you are ready to cook, preheat the oven to 150°C fan/170°C/325°F/gas 3. Toast the coriander, cumin and fennel seeds in a dry pan until fragrant and roughly crush in a pestle and mortar (or spice grinder). Stir in the oregano and ground coffee.

3.   Set the casserole dish over a medium-low heat and add a thin layer of vegetable oil. Generously coat the short ribs in the spice mix (keeping any excess aside) and add them to the pan (I do this in batches). Sear the ribs on the three meaty sides, taking your time until each is golden, around 5 minutes per side. Resist the temptation to turn the heat up to high – take your time. Once all the ribs have been seared, set aside.

4.   Drain off any excess oil from the pan, then add the whole peeled shallots, chilli powder, bay leaves, garlic, ginger, cinnamon stick and a generous pinch of salt. Cook over a low-medium heat until softened, around 10 minutes. Stir in any excess crushed spices, along with the ancho chilli, cooking for another 2 minutes until fragrant. Add the tomato paste and cook for a further minute. Deglaze the pan with the Corona beer and chicken or beef stock, scraping any browned bits from the bottom. Add the short ribs back into the pan in a single layer (they can be on their sides, if your pan is on the smaller side) and bring to a simmer.

5.   Cover with a cartouche (a circle of greaseproof paper with a small hole in the centre), then the casserole lid and bake in the oven for 3 hours. Turn the heat down to 130°C fan/150°C/300°F/gas 2 after the first hour, then remove the lid at the 2½ hour point.

6.   Meanwhile, prepare your pickled onions. Place the onions in a sieve (fine mesh strainer) and pour a kettle of boiled water over them. Shake any excess water off, then place them in a jar with the lime juice and a good pinch of sea salt. Make sure the onions are submerged in the lime juice, then leave until you're ready to eat. This is also a good time to remove the kernels from the corn (see Tip).

7.   Once the ribs have had their long stint in the oven, increase the oven temperature to 200°C fan/220°C/425°F/gas 7, remove the cartouche and cook for around 25 minutes until the tops of the ribs are starting to brown and the sauce has reduced to a thicker consistency. Season with the soy sauce and white balsamic vinegar.

8.   While the ribs are cooking at the higher temperature, make the corn polenta. Blitz the corn kernels to a rough purée with a stick blender (or food processor). Cook in a large frying pan until slightly thickened, then add the butter and salt. Season with freshly ground pepper.

9.   Serve the short ribs, family style, in the middle of the table alongside a bowl of the corn polenta sprinkled with the feta (if using), the quick-pickled onions and a crunchy green salad.

MAKE AHEAD

The short ribs can be made a day or two before, and gently reheated. The fresh corn polenta is best made just before serving.

TIP

The easiest and tidiest way to remove the kernels from corn is to get a large, wide bowl and then place a small bowl or ramekin, upturned, in the bottom. Rest one end of the corn on this upturned bowl and then run a knife down the sides of the cob to release the kernels.

tiramisu *tres leches* cake

Serves 8–12

100g (3½oz/generous ¾ cup) plain
    (all-purpose) flour
20g (¾oz/2½ tbsp) cornflour
    (cornstarch)
1 tsp baking powder
¼ tsp fine sea salt
3 eggs, separated
130g (4½oz/⅔ cup) caster (superfine)
    sugar
½ tsp vanilla bean paste
2 tbsp whole milk

for the coffee soak
230ml (8fl oz/scant 1 cup)
    evaporated milk
270g (9fl oz/generous 1 cup)
    sweetened condensed milk
235ml (8fl oz/scant 1 cup) whole milk
2 tbsp espresso powder
2–3 tbsp Kahlúa, to taste (optional)

for the topping
400ml (14fl oz/scant 1¾ cups) double
    (heavy) cream
1½ tbsp icing (confectioners') sugar
½ tsp vanilla bean paste
1 tsp cocoa powder

equipment
20cm (8in) non-stick loose-bottomed
    square tin
electric hand whisk

Cross tiramisu with the Latin American classic, a *tres leches* cake – a fatless sponge soaked in condensed, evaporated and normal milk (yep, ALL three) – and you get this. Despite the fact that it sounds extremely rich and heavy, it is actually light, summery, refreshing, even and moreish. If you like tiramisu, you'll adore this.

This cake requires an overnight stint in the fridge, so should be made the day before you want to serve.

1. Preheat the oven to 160°C fan/180°C/350°F/gas 4. Place a square of baking parchment in the bottom of the tin.

2. In a bowl, whisk together the flour, cornflour, baking powder and salt.

3. In a separate bowl, beat the egg whites using an electric hand whisk until soft peaks form. Add the sugar, a quarter at a time, beating well between each addition, until stiff peaks form. Add the vanilla, then the egg yolks, one at a time, beating thoroughly after each addition. Add the milk and beat until combined. Gently fold in the flour mixture, a third at a time.

4. Pour the batter into your prepared tin and bake for 18–20 minutes, or until a skewer comes out clean. Let the cake cool completely in the tin, then turn out and place it upside down to get a flat top.

5. In a large jug (or bowl) combine all the ingredients for the coffee soak. Use a wooden skewer to poke holes all over the cake and then pour three-quarters of the mixture over the cake, reserving the last quarter for serving. Place the cake in the fridge overnight, to give it time to absorb the coffee soak evenly.

6. Before serving, whip up the double cream with the icing sugar and vanilla until soft peaks form (be careful not to take it too far). Spread over the top of the cake, then dust with the cocoa powder. Serve the cake in squares, with the reserved coffee soak alongside.

coffee + biscoff no-bake cheesecake

Makes 8-12 slices

1 x 165g (5½oz) pack of light
    cream cheese
60g (2¼oz/⅔ cup) icing
    (confectioners') sugar
250g (9oz) smooth Biscoff spread
500ml (18fl oz/2 cups) double (heavy)
    cream, fridge cold
4 tsp espresso powder

for the biscuit base
60g (2¼oz/4 tbsp) coconut oil
30g (1oz) unsalted butter
25 Biscoff biscuits (about 200g/7oz),
    plus extra to serve

equipment
20cm (8in) springform tin
electric hand whisk
food processor (useful, but
    not essential)
chef's blowtorch (useful, but
    not essential)

TIP
When dealing with biscuit bases,
it can be helpful to build straight
onto the plate you want to serve
from – make sure your plate
is completely flat, then place
the ring of your springform
tin directly onto the plate
without the base, and build the
cheesecake as normal.

This cheesecake is inspired by my local ice cream kiosk, Minus 12. Their flavours change regularly, which keeps it exciting, but I'm always thrilled when I see the coffee Speculoos flavour on the board, as the bitterness of coffee balances the spiced, malty sweetness of the Biscoff. This cheesecake is pure, rich, unapologetic indulgence. Although I've presented this as a whole cheesecake, it would also work well served as little cheesecake pots in individual glasses.

All cheesecakes require an overnight stint in the fridge and this is no different: you won't get a clean(ish) slice from a set cheesecake unless you give it plenty of time to chill.

1. Start with the biscuit base. Melt together the coconut oil and butter, then set aside to cool slightly.

2. Add the Biscoff biscuits to a food processor and process briefly until you have a coarse crumb. Add the cooled coconut oil and butter mixture, pulse a few more times to combine, then tip into the tin. Alternatively, you can crush the biscuits by hand using a rolling pin and a sealable sandwich bag, and mix everything together in the pan that you melted the butter in. Press the mixture into the base of the tin, using a flat-bottomed glass to get it even. Chill in the fridge.

3. For the filling, whisk together the cream cheese and icing sugar until smooth. Separately, whisk together the Biscoff spread, double cream and espresso powder with an electric hand whisk until just combined. Fold the cream cheese into the Biscoff mix, then spoon this over the chilled biscuit base, smooth over the top and return to the fridge to set overnight.

4. To serve, release the cheesecake from the springform tin by applying a blowtorch to the sides. If you don't have a blowtorch, simply run a knife around the outside of the cheesecake instead. This is best served chilled, with each slice topped with a crumbled Biscoff biscuit.

coffee-pecan banana bread

Makes 8–10 slices

80g (3oz) roughly chopped pecans
(or walnuts)

3 overripe bananas (about
420g/14oz)

1 tsp vanilla bean paste

125g (4oz/generous ½ cup) light
muscovado (or light brown)
sugar

2 eggs

150ml (5fl oz/generous ½ cup)
vegetable (or sunflower) oil

150g (5oz/scant 1¼ cups) self-raising
flour

1 tsp ground cinnamon

½ tsp fine sea salt

2 tsp baking powder

2 tbsp instant espresso powder

2 tbsp demerara (turbinado) sugar

equipment
900g (2lb) loaf tin

Banana bread offers a double hit of sweetness from both sugar and overripe bananas, so the addition of some bitter coffee helps bring everything into balance. This is your morning treat and your morning coffee, rolled into one.

1. Preheat the oven to 160°C fan/180°C/350°F/gas 4. Grease or line your loaf tin.

2. Spread the pecans out on a baking tray and toast in the oven for 5–10 minutes while it heats up.

3. Peel and then mash the bananas with the vanilla, then whisk in the light muscovado sugar, followed by the eggs and oil.

4. In a separate bowl, mix together the flour, cinnamon, salt, baking powder and espresso powder, then whisk them into the banana mixture. Stir through the pecans.

5. Pour the batter into the lined loaf tin, then sprinkle over the demerara sugar. Bake for 50–60 minutes, or until an inserted skewer comes out fairly clean.

TIP
Never waste another moment of your life lining (or washing) a loaf tin: the loaf tin liners that you can buy in the big supermarkets are a game-changer.

mocha martini

Makes 2 cocktails

Who doesn't love an espresso martini? The ultimate pick-me-up before, during or after a night out, it gets even better with chocolate. The coffee beans to garnish your cocktail are entirely optional, but given that they symbolise health, wealth and happiness I tend to include them out of pure superstition.

1. Add the vodka, liqueur, coffee and cocoa bitters (if using) to a cocktail shaker. Fill the shaker with ice and shake vigorously for up to 1 minute (this is key to getting the froth). Taste and add more liqueur if you prefer it sweeter.

2. Strain into martini glasses and arrange three coffee beans in the centre of each cocktail. Serve immediately.

50ml (2fl oz/3 tbsp plus 1 tsp) high-quality vodka
70ml (2¾fl oz/¼ cup plus 2 tsp) crème de cacao liqueur
80ml (3fl oz/⅓ cup) freshly brewed espresso
dash or two of cocoa bitters (optional)
ice, for shaking
6 coffee beans, to garnish

equipment
cocktail shaker (or large jar)
cocktail strainer or small sieve (fine mesh strainer)
2 martini glasses (chilled is nice)

cocoa

I spent my entire childhood loathing chocolate, a tragic state of affairs that persisted until, aged twenty-two, I went to work for Pierre Hermé. I had long coveted his macarons but was dismayed to discover that he also sold a lot of chocolate. Working as a sales assistant in the *Galeries Lafayette*, I had to sample the entire chocolate collection in order to advise customers . . . Long story short: I was converted and have since been making up for lost time.

Before chocolate was a bar, it was a drink. Often described as a life-source and believed to date back to 3500 BC, it provided caffeine long before coffee and tea arrived on the scene. Initially consumed by the Mayo-Chinchipe-Marañón people (of modern-day Peru), and subsequently by indigenous Mesoamerican Indians (of modern-day Mexico/Central America), its long years on this planet translate to a colourful but tainted history which intersects key political and imperialist events, including the transatlantic slave trade.

The Mayans were the first to develop a rich chocolate culture, serving frothing cups of cocoa at weddings and births – and burying their dead with it. They believed cocoa was a heavenly food gifted by the serpent deity Kukulkan and used dried cocoa beans as a form of currency.

Spain was the first European country to be seduced by cocoa as a result of its colonial movements in Mesoamerica. When visiting the court of Montezuma, sixth emperor of the Aztec Empire, Spanish conquistadors were offered the drink and later, once they had conquered the Aztecs, they began to import cocoa beans to Europe. The indigenous origins of cocoa were originally cause for concern but perhaps it was the perceived danger that formed part of the attraction: cocoa was intoxicating, primal, sensual, forbidden . . . and very bitter. Soon enough it had been adopted by the Spanish royal court, sweetened with sugar and embellished with spices to temper its bitterness. It subsequently spread across Europe.

Cocoa transitioned from drink to bar in the mid-nineteenth century during the Industrial Revolution, driven by the invention of the cocoa press. The ability to separate the cocoa bean's natural fat (cocoa butter), leaving behind pure cocoa mass in powder form, made it possible to mix cocoa into drinks or recombine it with cocoa butter and sugar to make chocolate. And once condensed milk was added to the mix, the milk chocolate bar was born. By the beginning of the twentieth century, Milton Hershey was investing in the world's largest chocolate manufacturing facility in the US and chocolate had hit the big time.

During the nineteenth century, the cultivation of cocoa shifted to West Africa (in lieu of Africans being moved as slaves to South/Central American cocoa plantations). Processing cocoa beans was a laborious job, and as chocolate became increasingly popular across the world, greater demand fuelled the abuse of African people. Horrific abuses of human rights (slavery, child labour) continue to this day: not everything about chocolate is sweet. But slave-free chocolate does exist and it is our responsibility to, wherever we can, spend more on our chocolate to ensure that everyone in the supply chain is treated fairly. Brands to shop include Lucocoa, Hotel Chocolat, Divine, Seed & Bean, Montezuma's and Ombar.

That 4.5 million tonnes of cocoa are produced every year might trick you into believing that cocoa grows easily when, in fact, cocoa trees are fussy about the conditions they grow in (hence the 'cocoa belt', which runs just 20 degrees north and south of the equator). But beyond production and harvest, there is plenty more process: the beans are dried, roasted, ground, refined, tempered, poured and set into chocolate bars. The Maillard reaction (caramelisation) during the roasting process helps develop the flavour of the chocolate. Roasted beans then become cocoa nibs, which are subsequently ground into a smooth peanut-butter-like paste to be combined with sugar, cocoa butter and milk. The heat of the process results in melted chocolate that is voluptuous, thick and shiny. Finally, the chocolate is tempered, which involves taking it through specific temperature levels to control the transition from liquid to solid, ensuring a shiny finish and the right snap.

As a result of these complex processes, the flavour of chocolate varies hugely: it can be more or less bitter, fruity, wine-like, woody, earthy, spicy, resinous, smoky. And while good-quality chocolate is best appreciated without fuss, it pairs beautifully with many ingredients because of the complexity of its flavour profile. Nuts, spices and fruit are its most obvious bedfellows, but even ingredients like blue cheese can find a harmony.

I am a fan of 70% or 80% dark chocolate, where bitterness and sweetness are more likely to be in balance. But even chocolate bars within this range can vary because although the percentage tells you how high the total cocoa bean content is (relative to the amount of sugar), it doesn't tell you how much is cocoa *nibs* vs cocoa *butter*. Nibs are dark and bitter; cocoa butter is neutral and creamy. A 70% bar of chocolate with a high proportion of cocoa nibs will taste darker and more intense than a 70% bar with more cocoa butter, which is why it's worth trying different brands to establish your favourite.

If you're into baking with chocolate, then cocoa is a necessary ingredient, adding richness and intensity of colour to bakes. Buy the best quality you can get – it will reward you with depth of flavour. Another brilliant ingredient is cocoa nibs, which – as well as their pure, bitter flavour – have a distinctive knobbly texture. They are divine atop chocolate pots (page 206) and offer pops of bitterness and texture in the base of my cocoa nib tart (page 202).

Cocoa is one of the most nutrient-rich foods on the planet, but many of its beneficial compounds are stripped out as it undergoes processing. Raw cocoa powder is probably the closest modern equivalent of what the Mesoamericans consumed, containing flavanols that support the heart; mineral magnesium, which supports the nervous system; and anandamide, which enhances pleasure in the brain. Today's chocolate could never be labelled a superfood, but those cups of frothing bitter cocoa that the Mayans and Aztecs used to consume? 'The bitter elixir of life' (as described in the novel *Chocolat*), surely.

chicken schnitzel with *mole poblano* salsa + plantain

Serves 2

1 large (or 2 small) chicken breasts
1 tsp fine sea salt
freshly ground black pepper
vegetable oil, for shallow-frying
25g (1oz) ghee (or clarified butter)
1 lime, halved, to serve

for the crumb coating

2 eggs
2 tbsp double (heavy) cream
50g (2oz/½ cup) golden
    breadcrumbs
½ tsp cumin seeds, lightly crushed
1 tsp dried oregano
½ tsp chipotle chilli powder (or
    cayenne pepper)
½ tsp ground cinnamon
¼ tsp ground nutmeg
¼ tsp cayenne pepper

for the *mole poblano* salsa

125g (4½oz) baby plum tomatoes,
    cut into quarters
2 spring onions (scallions), finely sliced
2 green jalapeño slices, from a jar,
    finely chopped
2½ tbsp rapeseed (canola) oil
½ small garlic clove, peeled and
    finely grated
juice of ½ lime
½ tsp maple syrup
¼ tsp chipotle chilli powder,
    or to taste
½ tsp fine salt
¼ tsp ground cinnamon
½ tsp dried oregano
½ tsp cocoa powder
pinch of ground cloves

for the plantain

2 tbsp vegetable oil
1 large ripe plantain (about
    200g/7oz), peeled, and sliced
    into 1cm (½in) thick coins
flaky sea salt

Mole is the Mexican word for 'sauce', and throughout the country you will find all sorts of versions with different spices and herbs. *Mole poblano* is a thick, savoury chilli and chocolate sauce from Puebla and the one most synonymous with *mole* outside of Mexico. Here, it's the inspiration for a fresh tomato salsa with added depth from spices, chipotle and chocolate. Plantain works perfectly alongside this, as its sweetness complements the bitterness of the spices.

For best results, marinate your (bashed out) chicken breast in the egg mixture the night before.

1.   Slice the chicken breast in half laterally, then place a piece of cling film (plastic wrap) over the top of each piece and use a meat tenderiser (or rolling pin) to bash the meat out thinly. Season with salt and pepper.

2.   For the crumb coating: whisk the egg with the cream in one dish; mix the breadcrumbs and spices in another. Place the chicken pieces into the egg mixture and leave for 10 minutes, or ideally overnight.

3.   Meanwhile, make your salsa. Combine the tomatoes, spring onions and jalapeños in a small bowl with the rest of the ingredients. Check the seasoning and add more lime, salt or maple syrup to taste.

4.   Add the marinated chicken, piece by piece, to the spiced breadcrumbs and ensure they are well-coated.

5.   I'm going to ask you to multi-task here by cooking both the schnitzel and the plantain at the same time, because they both benefit from being served hot. So read the instructions for both, make sure everything is prepped, then get both your pans on and go!

6.   To cook the plantain, heat a pan over a medium heat and add the oil. Add the plantain, making sure not to overcrowd the pan, season with salt, and leave to fry until the bottoms are golden brown, 3–4 minutes. Flip over and repeat on the other sides. Drain on kitchen paper.

7.   To cook the schnitzel, place a deep wide frying pan (skillet) over a medium-high heat and fill with a 5mm (¼in) depth of oil. When the oil is hot enough (a breadcrumb added to the oil will turn golden), add the ghee or butter to the pan followed by the crumbed chicken pieces. Cook until golden brown on the bottom, around 3 minutes, then flip over and repeat on the other sides for another couple of minutes. Remove from the pan, briefly drain on kitchen paper, then serve with some of the salsa strewn across the top and the plantain and lime halves alongside.

prawns with chipotle, cocoa + charred pineapple

Serves 2 generously

½ tsp cocoa powder
½ tsp chipotle chilli powder
vegetable oil, for frying
350g (12oz) king prawns (jumbo
    shrimp), deveined (or peeled,
    if you prefer to eat your prawns
    without the fuss)
½ tsp fine sea salt
1 tbsp butter
2 garlic cloves, roughly chopped
15g (½oz) fresh root ginger, peeled
    and roughly chopped
½ Scotch bonnet chilli, deseeded
    and roughly chopped
½ very ripe pineapple, peeled,
    quartered, cored and chopped
    into 1cm (½in) slices
juice of ½ orange
1½ tsp soy sauce
juice of ½ lime
2 spring onions (scallions), finely sliced
10g (⅓oz) coriander (cilantro) leaves

Sweet prawns (shrimp), pineapple and orange juice are balanced here with spice from two types of chillies (Scotch bonnet, chipotle), acidity from lime and bitterness from cocoa. A colourful dish that requires you to get your hands dirty (in the best way).

1. Combine the cocoa and chipotle powder and set aside.

2. Heat a thin layer of oil in a wok or frying pan (skillet) until hot. Season the prawns with the salt, then fry for 1–2 minutes until they turn pink and crispy. Remove with a slotted spoon and set aside to drain on kitchen paper.

3. In a separate frying pan, melt the butter over a medium heat, then add the garlic, ginger and Scotch bonnet. Add the pineapple pieces and fry until they start to gain some colour, then add the orange juice and soy and allow most of it to evaporate off. Add the prawns back to the pan and briefly toss through to warm back up.

4. Plate up, squeeze over the lime, garnish with spring onions and coriander, and dust over the cocoa/chilli powder mix.

aubergine *caponata*, reinvented

Serves 4-6

3 tbsp golden (or standard) sultanas
(or raisins)

4 tbsp white balsamic vinegar

2 large aubergines (eggplants),
sliced

4 tbsp olive oil, plus extra for brushing

fine sea salt

4 anchovies

1 large white onion, finely sliced

2 celery sticks, very finely sliced

½ small–medium courgette (zucchini),
finely diced

2 tsp capers

2 medium plum tomatoes,
finely diced

2 tbsp pine nuts, toasted

2 tbsp grated dark chocolate
(minimum 70% cocoa solids,
but 100% is ideal)

½ bunch of flat-leaf parsley,
leaves picked

There are examples the world over of the brilliant combination that is aubergine and tomatoes: Italian *melanzane* (see my fusion version on page 130) and *pasta alla norma*, Turkish *soslu patlıcan*, French aubergine *à la Provençale*, Moroccan *zaalouk*, Persian aubergine *chermoula*, *brinjal* curries from Sri Lanka, Greek *melitzanosalata*. These two ingredients seem to belong together. Here they appear in a Sicilian dish, *caponata*, that is the very definition of balancing flavours: sweetness from the tomatoes and sultanas (golden raisins), acidity from the tomatoes (again) and vinegar, bitterness from celery and dark chocolate (yes, really – this is traditional!) and salt from the capers and anchovies (my addition).

Caponata is typically half stew, half relish, but my version is slightly deconstructed for something lighter and prettier. It makes a great side dish to baked or steamed white fish, or a roasted joint of meat.

1. Preheat the oven to 220°C fan/240°C/475°F/gas 9.

2. Add the golden sultanas and white balsamic vinegar to a small dish or glass and set aside to soak.

3. Spread the aubergine slices over two large baking trays lined with greaseproof paper and brush both sides with olive oil, then season with half a teaspoon of salt. Roast in the oven for 20–25 minutes until golden brown, then remove and leave to cool.

4. Meanwhile, heat a large saucepan over a medium heat, then add 2 tablespoons of the olive oil along with the anchovies. Cook until the anchovies have fully broken down, then add the onion along with a decent pinch of salt. Stir to coat the onion in the anchovy oil, cover with a lid and cook for 10–15 minutes, allowing the onions to soften and turn translucent (a little colour is fine). Next, add the celery and courgette, another generous pinch of salt and the remaining 2 tablespoons of olive oil. Replace the lid of the pan and cook for a further 10 minutes until softened. Add the capers, soaked sultanas and tomatoes and cook for another 5 minutes.

5. To serve, arrange the roasted aubergine slices on a platter, then dollop spoonfuls of the onion mixture in and among the slices. Sprinkle over the pine nuts, grated chocolate and parsley. This is best served at room temperature.

cocoa nib tart, three ways

Serves 10–12

for the cocoa nib base

180g (6oz) ginger nut biscuits
    (18–20 biscuits)
40g (1½oz) cocoa nibs
2 tbsp cocoa powder
½ tsp ground cinnamon
¼ tsp fine salt
60g (2¼oz) coconut oil, melted

for the chocolate
cream filling

1 gelatine sheet
200ml (7fl oz/scant 1 cup) whole milk
½ tsp fine sea salt
200g (7oz) dark cooking chocolate,
    finely chopped
110g (4¼oz) butter
110g (4¼oz/½ cup plus 1 tbsp) sugar
1 egg yolk

for the flavoured layer
(optional, see
introduction)

100g (3½oz) Grapefruit Marmalade
    (page 46)/store-bought salted
    caramel sauce/store-bought
    morello cherry compote

for the chocolate shell
(optional)

110ml (3¾fl oz/scant ½ cup)
    neutral oil
150g (5oz) dark cooking chocolate

equipment

food processor
20cm (8in) sandwich cake tin
blowtorch (helpful, but not essential)

This is a pick-your-own-tart situation – which is to say that, while you do need to be a chocolate lover to enjoy this, you can tweak the recipe to suit your palate. The basis of this recipe is a delicious ginger nut chocolate base, over which you pour a luscious, glossy chocolate cream inspired by the French dessert *St Emilion au chocolat*. I often find chocolate ganache tarts simply too rich and intense, but this chocolate filling is gentler and more unctuous. Under that cream, there is a surprise layer and this is where I invite you to play. Any hardcore bitter fan should spread a layer of marmalade. More of a sweet tooth? Opt for salted caramel instead. A lover of Black Forest gateaux? A morello cherry compote would work beautifully here. In fact, the options are endless: have fun with it (or keep it simple and leave the extra layer out).

1. Bloom your gelatine for the chocolate cream filling by adding it to a small bowl of cold water. Set aside.

2. For the cocoa nib base, add all the ingredients except the coconut oil to a food processor and pulse to a coarse crumb. Pour the melted coconut oil through the funnel and pulse at the same time until you have a wet, sandy mixture. Line the base of the cake tin with greaseproof paper, tip in the mixture and use a flat-bottomed glass to press it into the bottom and up the sides of the tin slightly (you want there to be a 1cm (½in) lip to keep the filling contained). Chill in the fridge.

3. For the filling, warm the milk and salt in a small saucepan until steaming. Remove the gelatine leaf from the cold water and squeeze gently to remove the excess water, then whisk into the warm milk. Remove from the heat and add the chocolate, stir until fully melted, then set aside to cool slightly.

4. Meanwhile, cream the butter and the sugar together until well combined. Beat in the egg yolk thoroughly, then stir in the melted chocolate and milk mixture until smooth and glossy.

5. If using, spoon your chosen surprise layer into the base and spread it out until you have an even layer. Cover with the chocolate cream filling and leave to set for at least 3–4 hours.

6. Once set, make the chocolate shell topping (if making). Heat the oil in a pan until warm, then stir in the chocolate until melted. Allow to cool to room temperature (but not cold), then pour over the top of the tart and return it to the fridge to set for 1 hour.

7. To serve, if you have a blowtorch, apply heat around the tin to help it release neatly; otherwise, you can simply run a knife around the tart to release the sides. The tart is best sliced cold directly from the fridge and slices left for 5–10 minutes to take the chill off. To ensure a clean cut, wipe your knife after each slice and, if you have a blowtorch, heat the blade slightly ahead of each cut.

TIP

When dealing with biscuit bases, it can be helpful to build straight onto the plate you want to serve from – make sure your plate is completely flat, then place the ring of your springform tin directly onto the plate without the base, and build the rest as normal.

bitter chocolate torte with passionfruit sauce

Serves 6-8

150g (5oz) butter, cut into large cubes, plus extra for greasing

180g (6oz) dark chocolate (65% cocoa solids), roughly chopped or broken up into squares

3 eggs, separated

105g (4oz/½ cup) caster (superfine) sugar

2 tbsp dark rum (I like Mount Gay Black Barrel)

½ tsp fine sea salt (if your butter is slightly salted) or 1 tsp (if using unsalted butter)

30g (1oz/¼ cup) cocoa powder, sifted

whipped cream, to serve

for the passionfruit sauce

18 passionfruits

6 tbsp caster (superfine) sugar

equipment

20cm (8in) sandwich cake tin

electric hand mixer

food processor

TIP

When working with mixtures that can split (the chocolate batter, in this case), they can often be saved by whisking in 1–2 tbsp of freshly boiled water.

This torte is best made the day before you want to eat it, as the flavours and textures improve after they've had proper time to rest. The torte and passionfruit sauce are delicious without any further adornments, but you can also serve this with a dollop of softly whipped cream alongside. I like to serve slices of this torte with a generous quantity of passionfruit sauce, so I find the quantity here enough to serve around half to two-thirds of the torte.

1. Preheat the oven to 170°C fan/190°C/375°F/gas 5. Grease and line the base of the cake tin.

2. Melt the butter in a pan over a very low heat, then add the chocolate and allow it to melt into the butter (this ensures the chocolate doesn't burn in any way). Alternatively, melt the chocolate and butter for 1 minute in a microwave. Once fully melted and glossy, leave to cool for 10 minutes.

3. Whisk together the egg yolks and sugar until fluffy and pale, at least 3–5 minutes with an electric hand mixer. Gently fold in the melted chocolate mixture until there are no streaks in the batter, then fold in the rum and salt. Next, sift the cocoa powder over the mixture and fold in.

4. In a separate bowl, whisk up the egg whites to the soft peak stage, then fold into the batter. Pour the batter into your prepared tin, then place in the oven and reduce the heat to 150°C fan/170°C/325°F/gas 3. Bake for 15–17 minutes, then allow to cool and set overnight.

5. For the passionfruit sauce, scoop out the pulp of the passionfruits into a food processor and blitz just to loosen the seeds. Strain through a sieve (fine mesh strainer) into a saucepan (using the back of the spoon to make sure you get all the passionfruit pulp through) and add the sugar. Set over a medium heat and cook for 2–3 minutes until the sugar has melted and the sauce has thickened slightly and is glossy.

6. This is best served on a plate with a rim or a lip so that the sauce remains contained. Flood the plate with a thin layer of the passionfruit sauce, then place a slice of the chocolate torte in the middle with a soft dollop of whipped cream alongside.

boozy prune chocolate pots

Makes 8

6 egg yolks (see Food Waste)
350ml (12fl oz/1½ cups) double (heavy) cream
200ml (7fl oz/scant 1 cup) whole milk
200g (7oz) dark chocolate, chopped into small pieces
75g (3oz/generous ⅓ cup) caster (superfine) sugar
½ tsp flaky sea salt, or to taste
1 tsp vanilla bean paste

for the boozy prunes
16 pitted prunes
60ml (2½fl oz/4 tbsp) brandy
150ml (5fl oz/⅔ cup) hot double-strength Earl Grey tea

to serve
150ml (5fl oz/⅔ cup) double (heavy) cream
cocoa nibs or sifted cocoa powder

equipment
8 ramekins

FOOD WASTE
Egg whites freeze well. Or you can use them immediately in meringues (see page 50 for the Individual Negroni Pavlovas), *financiers* or *langues de chats*.

MAKE AHEAD
The chocolate pots will last up to 3 days in the fridge. The prunes can be steeped up to a week ahead – simply steep them in the tea/brandy mixture, allow them to cool, then place in the fridge in a sealed container.

Chocolate pots are to dinner party desserts what the LBD (Little Black Dress) is to a woman's wardrobe: easy, fool-proof, ever-reliable . . . but no less sexy for it. This recipe is perfect when you want to end the meal with something classic, chocolatey, chic. It also offers a little surprise element (enter: secret boozy prunes in the bottom).

These are easy to rustle up on the day or make ahead (see note below) – if opting for the former, simply factor in the hour or so that they need to set in the fridge.

1. Start with the boozy prunes by adding the prunes and brandy to a bowl, then pour over the hot Earl Grey tea and set aside to steep (the longer the better!).

2. To make the chocolate pots, whisk the egg yolks in a small bowl. Heat the 350ml cream and the milk in a saucepan over a medium heat until hot. Add a third of the hot milk mixture to the yolks and whisk until smooth, then add this mixture to the pan, whisking to ensure everything is combined. Immediately reduce the heat to low and whisk until the mixture thickens, around 1–2 minutes.

3. Remove the pan from the heat and add the chocolate and sugar, whisking until melted. Strain through a fine sieve (fine mesh strainer) into a large (1 litre/1 quart) jug or medium bowl. Add the salt and vanilla, and stir to combine. Taste and season with more salt if you think it needs it.

4. Place a couple of boozy prunes in the base of each ramekin or serving glass, then divide the chocolate mixture among the 8 ramekins. Refrigerate until set – around an hour. (The remaining brandy and tea mixture can be discarded or, preferably, used in a hot toddy.)

5. Remove the chocolate pots from the fridge 30–45 minutes before serving so that they can come to room temperature. To serve, whip the remaining cream until soft peaks are achieved. Add a teaspoon or so of whipped cream to the top of each chocolate pot and garnish with a few cocoa nibs or a little sifted cocoa powder (garnishing with both is, of course, also acceptable).

black *velvet* cake

Serves 12 generously

100g (3½oz) dark cooking chocolate (55% cocoa solids), finely chopped
100ml (3½fl oz/scant ½ cup) hot, strong coffee
320g (11½oz/2½ cups) plain (all-purpose) flour
120g (4½oz/generous 1 cup) cocoa powder
2 tsp bicarbonate of soda (baking soda)
½ tsp baking powder
450g (1lb/2¼ cups) caster (superfine) sugar
1 tsp fine sea salt
3 large eggs
1 tsp vanilla bean paste
300ml (10fl oz/1¼ cups) buttermilk
450ml (15fl oz/1¾ cups) vegetable oil

for the malted cream cheese icing
250g (9oz) butter, softened
3 tbsp malt extract
200g (7oz/2 cups) icing (confectioners') sugar
2 x 340g (12oz) packs of full-fat cream cheese

equipment
whisk or electric hand mixer
2 x 20cm (8in) sandwich cake tins

At the risk of making enemies, I have never understood the excitement around red velvet cake. The cake itself has always tasted bland to me – and although it technically contains cocoa powder, 1–2 tablespoons of the stuff does not a chocolate cake make. It feels like the popularity of red velvet cake has always been about the icing and it's made me wonder: couldn't we just put the cream cheese icing on a nicer, more legitimately chocolatey cake? The answer is yes. This cake is what I've always wanted red velvet to be: it's still light, multi-layered and sandwiched with a luscious icing, but the cake layers have a proper amount of cocoa in them, the garish red food colouring has been dropped and the icing is malted. Let me introduce you to black velvet cake – red velvet cake's grown-up sibling.

This cake keeps well in the fridge and is actually decent cold, but is even better brought to room temperature before eating. You can also warm up individual slices slightly and drizzle with cream.

1. Preheat the oven to 160°C fan/180°C/350°F/gas 4.

2. Combine the chocolate and coffee in a jug and stir until melted.

3. In a bowl, sift together the flour, cocoa, bicarbonate of soda and baking powder, then add the sugar and salt, and whisk together.

4. In a large bowl, whisk the eggs for 5 minutes until thickened and pale. Stir through the vanilla, buttermilk and vegetable oil until combined, then whisk in the dry ingredients.

5. Divide the batter between the sandwich tins and bake for 30 minutes, or until an inserted skewer comes out clean. Remove from the oven and allow to cool completely.

6. Meanwhile, make the icing. In a medium bowl, whisk together the butter, malt extract and icing sugar until smooth and fluffy. Separately, whisk the cream cheese briefly until smooth, then fold into the butter mix. Store in the fridge until you want to assemble the cake.

7. When the sponges are completely cool, use a bread knife or cake leveller to slice each in half to create 4 layers. You can wrap these in cling film (plastic wrap) if you're not going to use them immediately.

8. To assemble the cake, place a sponge layer on your serving dish, then spread with a quarter of the cream cheese icing. Repeat with the remaining sponge layers, topping off with the neatest layer of sponge you have. Swirl the last quarter of the icing over the top, then place in the fridge to set for 20–30 minutes.

saint lucia cocoa tea

Serves 2

500ml (17fl oz/generous 2 cups) water
2 bay leaves, torn in half
4 cloves
¼ nutmeg, grated
1 cinnamon stick, broken in half
pinch of fine sea salt
25g (1oz) Saint Lucia cocoa stick,
    grated
200ml (7fl oz/scant 1 cup)
    evaporated milk
1½ tbsp sugar, or to taste
1½ tsp cornflour (cornstarch)

Saint Lucian cocoa tea is the best hot chocolate you'll ever taste – and yet it's not like any other hot chocolate. First, a spiced infusion is made with bay leaves, cinnamon and nutmeg, and then you grate in cocoa stick – a dark, compacted, dry mass of roasted, deshelled and crushed cocoa beans that delivers pure unadorned bitterness. Evaporated milk is added to soothe, and sugar to sweeten, until you have the perfect balance. It's a drink often served at breakfast with fried bakes (a slightly sweetened bread) and it is the essence of comfort.

It is possible to order Saint Lucian cocoa sticks online and I urge you to try the real deal – however, cocoa powder can be used in a pinch: use 2 tablespoons of cocoa powder, increase the sugar slightly and add a pinch of salt.

1. Combine the water, spices and salt in a pan, bring to the boil, then simmer gently for 15 minutes to create a spiced infusion.

2. Add the grated cocoa stick to the infusion and simmer for a further 10 minutes. Add the evaporated milk and sweeten with sugar to taste, then simmer for another 5 minutes. Finally, in a small glass or bowl whisk the cornflour with a small measure of the chocolate liquid until there are no lumps, then add this paste to the saucepan and stir to make sure it's dispersed. Simmer for a final 2-3 minutes, then strain and serve immediately.

liquorice

In ancient Greek texts, there are numerous mentions of a plant, *glukurrhiza*, used to ease asthma, reduce inflammation and even combat sterility. Although we are accustomed to thinking of medicine as tasting unpleasant and often bitter, *glukurrhiza* translates to 'sweet root' – because it is, in fact, fifty times sweeter than sugar. We're talking of liquorice root; a hardy perennial herb from the pea family whose soft roots can grow as deep as the plant grows high. Its use pervades world history: Julius Caesar fed it to his troops to alleviate thirst; the ancient Chinese used liquorice in religious ceremonies and medicinal preparations; and the ancient Egyptians buried Tutankhamun with a hoard of liquorice roots. And yet, is there any food on the planet more divisive than this one?

Liquorice is nature's dark, complex candy, with a flavour so distinct it could never please everyone – it doesn't even try. The world cleaves into liquorice lovers and liquorice loathers. Perhaps one of the challenges with liquorice is that it refuses to be tied down: it is both bitter and sweet, harsh and soft, metallic and earthy, medicinal and caramel-like. Sometimes liquorice is mimicked with anise, but true aficionados know that authenticity can only be found in the ground root of the liquorice plant, which is uniquely complex in flavour.

I didn't grow up loving liquorice. My earliest memories of the stuff are of my grandfather eating Liquorice Allsorts and, although I didn't hate them, I was far more inclined to try to steal his Bakewell Slices. It wasn't until adulthood that I came to appreciate that my love of aniseed flavours (fennel, basil, caraway and so on) might stretch to liquorice.

I'll admit that liquorice can be overwhelming, but learning to work with it can yield some exquisite results. It's helpful to know that it can be toned down by cream or balanced by sharp flavours, such as blackcurrant and lemon (the latter being a favourite of the Swedes). Liquorice and blackcurrant first appeared as a combination in those old-fashioned boiled sweets, but I love this flavour combination in a fruit galette (see page 222). Or try the quick, cheat's doughnuts on page 224, with a lemon cream that beautifully balances the intense liquorice sugar.

Liquorice's natural sweetness means that it loves salt, and salted varieties of liquorice are particularly popular in Finland. Finnish fans will argue that the salt brings the other flavours into harmony – like a more complex salted caramel – but I'm prepared to accept that it may simply come down to Finnish *sisu*: a stoic determination in the face of challenging things.

Although we now live in an interconnected world where we can summon many foodstuffs at the click of a button, it remains true that cuisines typically develop around the ingredients that are locally and readily available, yet liquorice is an anomaly in this regard. The liquorice plant originated in warm climes and is now typically cultivated around the Med in countries such as Spain, Italy, Turkey, Greece and Georgia, as well as the Middle East. However, it is most popular in more northern European countries: Scandinavia, where there is a cult-like following that extends to Comic Con-style liquorice festivals; Iceland, where most candy bars contain black liquorice and liquorice soft serve is pretty common; as well as the Netherlands, Germany and the UK (which once had its own liquorice industry). Although it's hard to know why liquorice has taken such a strong hold over these particular cultures, somehow it seems to make sense that this dense, opaque, black substance would pair with cold climates.

Like grapefruit, bitter leaves, walnuts, cocoa and coffee, liquorice has some remarkable health properties. It has been reported to be anti-inflammatory, antiviral, anti-ulcer, anti-carcinogenic. Yet it is also dark and dangerous: the sweet-tasting substance, glycyrrhizin, found in true liquorice root, is capable of inducing high blood pressure and irregular heart rhythms. The NHS warns against eating more than 57g of black liquorice a day for risk of 'potentially serious health problems'. But liquorice doesn't feel like a daily habit kind of food to me: I think of it as something to savour occasionally in moments of dark devotion.

liquorice miso-glazed aubergine

Serves 2-4

2 aubergines (eggplants)
2 tbsp vegetable oil
2 spring onions (scallions), finely
    sliced, to garnish
sesame seeds, toasted, to garnish

for the glaze
1 tbsp white miso
½ tsp caster (superfine) sugar
2 tsp sake
1 tsp tamari (or soy sauce)
1 tsp sesame oil (or ½ tsp toasted
    sesame oil)
¼ tsp fine liquorice powder

Miso aubergine is a crowd-pleaser (and one of the best ways to eat this vegetable). Here, I add liquorice, which brings a bittersweet note that plays off against the darker, umami flavours of soy and miso. This is an adaptation of a Milli Taylor recipe and it's a versatile dish that can be served alongside sushi rice and tenderstem broccoli for a light lunch, or alongside meat or fish for dinner.

1. Preheat the oven to 190°C fan/210°C/425°F/gas 7.

2. Cut each aubergine in half lengthways, then score the flesh quite deeply (without piercing through the skin) to create a cross-hatched pattern. Brush each half with the oil, then place on a baking tray and bake in the oven for 15–20 minutes until starting to develop some colour.

3. Meanwhile, make the glaze by whisking together all the ingredients in a small bowl.

4. Remove the aubergines from the oven and brush over the glaze, then return to the oven for another 15 minutes until caramelised and deeply golden.

5. Allow the aubergines to cool for around 5 minutes, then scatter over the spring onions and sesame seeds and serve. I prefer to eat just the flesh, leaving the skin behind.

soy + liquorice chicken

Serves 4-6

4 chicken legs
juice of 1 lime
1 fresh lime, halved, to garnish

for the marinade

2 tbsp Kewpie mayonnaise
60g (2¼oz/scant ¼ cup) runny honey
1½ tsp fine liquorice powder
2 tbsp Shaoxing rice wine
1 tbsp grated fresh root ginger
100ml (3½fl oz/scant ½ cup) tamari
(or soy sauce)

This is an easy chicken dinner perfect for a weeknight or weekend meal. It is lovely served with some rice, steamed greens (such as bok or pak choi), sliced spring onions (scallions) and toasted sesame seeds.

If you can marinate the chicken overnight, that's ideal.

1. Make the marinade. In a jug, combine the mayonnaise, honey and liquorice powder and whisk until smooth. Whisk in the rice wine and ginger, then gradually whisk in the tamari until you have a smooth, fairly liquid marinade.

2. Place the chicken in a snug-fitting roasting tin and pour over the marinade, using your hands (or some tongs) to ensure the chicken is fully coated. Cover and place in the fridge for a couple of hours, or overnight.

3. When you are ready to cook, preheat the oven to 220°C fan/240°C/ 475°F/gas 9.

4. Add the lime juice to the marinated chicken, then roast in the oven for 40–45 minutes until the skin is well charred.

5. Remove from the oven and set aside to rest for at least 10 minutes.

6. To serve, place the chicken legs in a deep-ish bowl, then pour the cooking juices in and around the chicken (avoid the skin as you want this to stay crispy). Squeeze over half a lime and serve the other half alongside.

braised pork shoulder with ginger + liquorice

Serves 6-8

vegetable oil, for searing the pork

1.5kg (3lb) pork shoulder, crackling fat removed and discarded if included on the joint

300g (10½oz) shallots, finely sliced

35g (1½oz) fresh root ginger, grated

8 garlic cloves, grated

4 tbsp *kecap manis* (Indonesian sweet soy sauce)

4 tbsp light soy sauce

2 tbsp tamarind paste

800ml (1⅓ pints/scant 3½ cups) chicken stock

100g (3½oz) soft liquorice, chopped

3 red chillies, deseeded and finely chopped

1–1½ tbsp rice wine vinegar, to taste

equipment

stick blender

casserole dish (Dutch oven)

TIP

I swear by using a cartouche whenever I'm slow-cooking something (particularly meat) – it helps ensure that whatever you're making cooks uniformly and quickly. See also the Porter Beef Shin Ragu (page 108) and the Ancho Coffee Short Ribs (page 182).

This is a sweet, sour and sticky slow-braised pork dish that, in using liquorice, plays on the flavours of Chinese five spice. Adapted from a Diana Henry recipe (from her wonderful book *How to Eat a Peach*), there are multiple ways you could eat this: over rice or noodles, or in lettuce cups.

1. Heat a thin layer of vegetable oil in a heavy-based casserole dish (Dutch oven) over a medium heat. Add the pork and sear until golden all over, then set aside.

2. Preheat the oven to 160°C fan/180°C/350°F/gas 4.

3. Add the shallots to the casserole dish, along with a splash more oil if needed, and cook for about 10 minutes until soft and translucent, then stir through the ginger and garlic and cook for a minute or two. Add the *kecap manis*, soy sauce, tamarind and stock, then bring to the boil. Add the liquorice and chillies, and simmer for around 5 minutes until the liquorice has softened, then use a stick blender to blend the liquid until smooth.

4. Add the pork shoulder back to the casserole dish, cover with a cartouche (a circle of baking paper with a small hole in the middle) and the lid, then cook in the oven for 3 hours, removing the lid for the last hour of cooking time.

5. Remove from the oven and allow to cool slightly before skimming off any excess fat and adding the vinegar, to taste. Shred the pork with a fork and mix it through the sauce.

blackcurrant, blueberry + liquorice galette

Serves 8

300g (10½oz) fresh blueberries
100g (3½oz) fresh (or frozen)
    blackcurrants
3 tbsp caster (superfine) sugar
1½ tsp fine liquorice powder
1½ tbsp cornflour (cornstarch)
1 tbsp fresh lemon juice
1 quantity of Pie Dough
    (see page 231)
1 tbsp whole milk
1 tbsp demerara (turbinado) sugar
single (light) cream, to serve

equipment
large baking tray

I love a galette – they're comforting, fruit-forward and effortless. This combination of flavours is beautiful – the blueberries offer sweetness, the blackcurrants much-needed sharpness and the liquorice a deeper, more complex flavour that matches the gorgeous deep purple stains of the berries. You can absolutely buy ready-made pastry for this, but I do encourage you to make the pastry yourself – it's surprisingly fun and the flavour is unmatched. To serve, cold single (light) cream is essential.

1. Preheat the oven to 170°C fan/190°C/375°F/gas 5. Line the baking tray with greaseproof paper.

2. Combine the fruit in a bowl.

3. In a glass, whisk together the sugar, liquorice powder and cornflour. Add to the fruit and mix, then stir through the lemon juice. Set aside.

4. Roll out the pastry to 4mm (¼in) thick, then cut out a 30cm (12in) diameter circle and transfer this to the lined baking tray. Place the fruit filling in the middle of the pastry disc, leaving a 3cm (1in) border around the edge, then fold the pastry in over the fruit all the way around. Brush the pastry edges with the milk, then sprinkle them with the demerara sugar and bake for around 1 hour until deeply golden.

5. Allow to cool for 10 minutes before serving with a pour of cream.

TAKE IT EASY
It won't beat homemade flaky pastry, but when you want something quick and easy, this works perfectly well with store-bought puff pastry (please buy the best quality that you can, ideally made with butter) – simply halve the filling quantity, as store-bought is smaller than the Pie Dough recipe.

TIP
A tip from Alison Roman, when it comes to baking anything with pie dough: it always needs a lot longer in the oven than you think it will. You'll be tempted to remove this galette halfway through the cooking time, but you'll be rewarded if you hold out. See also the Cranberry and Pear Pie on page 150.

liquorice + lemon *zeppole* doughnuts

Makes 15-20

for the doughnuts
2 eggs
zest of 1 lemon
2 tbsp caster (superfine) sugar
200g (7oz) ricotta, strained
2 tsp baking powder
¼ tsp fine sea salt
100g (3½oz/scant 1 cup) plain
    (all-purpose) flour
vegetable oil, for deep-frying

for the liquorice sugar
2 tbsp caster (superfine) sugar
½ tsp fine liquorice powder (or
    ground cinnamon)

for the lemon cream
juice of 1 lemon (60ml/4 tbsp)
2 eggs
75g (3oz/generous ⅓ cup) caster
    (superfine) sugar
pinch of salt
110g (4¼oz) butter

equipment
food processor
temperature probe or deep-fat fryer
    (not essential, but very helpful)

It was thanks to a lovely lady from Sweden, Lis, who I met on my way to visit the Lakrids liquorice factory in Copenhagen, that I came to discover that Swedes love the combination of liquorice and lemon. As soon as I tried it I was sold: the lemon does a great job of cutting through the intensity of the liquorice. I'd even go as far as to say that it almost cancels it out, which makes this a great recipe for those who are less enamoured with liquorice. Bonus: these yeast-free doughnuts take only 5 minutes to mix up, so you can have doughnuts ready in just 45 minutes (including the resting time).

The lemon cream is a recipe I learned when working for Pierre Hermé in Paris, which I have adapted slightly, and it is glorious: light, silky, creamy and with a real clarity of lemon flavour. In Pierre Hermé's patisseries they use it to fill their lemon tarts, but it works beautifully on its own as a sort of lemon pudding – or here, as an accompaniment to the doughnuts.

Make sure to strain the ricotta in advance.

1.   Start with the liquorice sugar. In a medium bowl, combine the caster sugar and liquorice powder (or cinnamon). Set aside.

2.   For the doughnut batter, whisk together the eggs and lemon zest, then add the sugar and whisk thoroughly. Add the ricotta and whisk again, then sprinkle (or sift) over the baking powder, salt and flour, and whisk until just incorporated. Set the batter aside to rest, either in the fridge or – if it's not too warm – at room temperature.

3.   Meanwhile, make the lemon cream. Prepare a bain-marie – set a bowl over a pan of gently simmering water, ensuring that the base of the bowl does not touch the water. Add the lemon juice and eggs to the bowl and whisk together, then whisk in the sugar and salt. Whisk continuously until the mixture thickens and all bubbles subside, around 10 minutes. Set aside to cool for 5 minutes, while you cut your butter into 1.5cm (¾in) cubes.

4.   Transfer the cooled egg mixture to the small bowl of a food processor and start to process, adding the cubes of butter down the funnel one at a time, waiting until the previous one is fully incorporated before adding another. In my experience, it's best to replace the chute cover in between butter cubes, as otherwise the mixture can spit out and cause a mess. When all the butter has been incorporated you should have a pale lemon cream. Transfer to a jar or container and store in the fridge so that it firms up.

5.   To cook the doughnuts, heat enough vegetable oil for deep-frying in a deep, heavy pan or deep-fat fryer to 160°C (320°F). Cook the doughnuts in 2–3 batches, as it's best not to overcrowd the pan. Carefully drop teaspoonfuls (no bigger!) of the batter into the oil and fry until they turn a deep-ish golden brown, around 5 minutes (they'll turn themselves over of their own accord). Remove with a slotted spoon to drain on kitchen paper, then toss in the liquorice sugar.

6.   Each doughnut should be eaten with a generous smear of the lemon cream, which is needed to balance out the intensity of the liquorice.

TIP

If you forgot to strain the ricotta, there is a quicker way, courtesy of J. Kenji López-Alt. Spread it out on a triple layer of kitchen paper, top with another triple layer of kitchen paper, then press down to help the paper absorb the excess moisture. The kitchen paper should peel right off.

pineapple, rum + liquorice upside-down cake

Serves 8–10

for the cake

200g (7oz/1½ cups plus 1 tbsp) plain (all-purpose) flour
2 tsp baking powder
½ tsp bicarbonate of soda (baking soda)
200g (7oz) lightly salted butter
200g (7oz/generous 1 cup) light muscovado sugar
4 eggs
75ml (scant ⅓ cup) dark rum (or whole milk, or the juice from tinned pineapple – see below)

for the caramelised pineapple

150g (5oz/¾ cup) granulated sugar
50g (2oz) butter
1½ tsp fine liquorice power (optional)
½ tsp flaky sea salt
1 medium–large pineapple, peeled, sliced into rings 7.5mm (⅜in) thick, cored and halved

equipment

23cm (9in) non-stick cake tin (not springform or loose-bottomed)
electric hand whisk

ALTERNATIVES

To make this with tinned pineapple, use 1 x 435g (15oz) tin of pineapple slices in juice. Pop the pineapple rings straight in the bottom of the cake tin and pour the caramel over the top (they'll disintegrate if you cook them in the caramel). Replace the rum with the juice from the tin, if preferred, and/or add a couple of tablespoons to the caramel for extra flavour.

This recipe is a more grown-up take on the classic pineapple upside-down cake, with liquorice in the caramel and a good slug of rum in the cake batter. The latter was inspired by a classic Bajan rum cake and, to be honest, I'm now wondering why I don't add rum to all my cakes. Both additions make the cake more interesting and nudge it into dessert territory. This is best served with double (heavy) cream.

1. Preheat the oven to 170°C fan/190°C/375°F/gas 5. Line the base of the cake tin with baking paper.

2. For the caramel, set a heavy-based pan over a medium-high heat. I recommend using a light-coloured pan so that you can see the colour. Sprinkle some of the granulated sugar across the bottom of the pan in a thin layer and wait until it starts to melt. When around half of the sugar layer has turned to a light caramel, add another layer of sugar and wait for that to start melting. Repeat until all the sugar has been used. Because this is a direct caramel (not a water-based one), you can stir it occasionally and bring the edges into the middle if they're melting unevenly. When all the sugar has melted and turned into a caramel, whisk in the butter (it may seize up, but keep going!), then sift in the liquorice powder (if using) and salt before whisking again.

3. Be very careful with this next step, as the caramel is extremely hot. Add the pineapple slices to the caramel and cook for around 5 minutes, flipping them over halfway through.

4. Arrange the pineapple slices in the bottom of the cake tin and pour the caramel over. Leave to cool for 5–10 minutes.

5. For the cake, sift together the flour, baking powder and bicarbonate of soda in a large bowl. Add the butter, muscovado sugar and eggs, then use an electric hand whisk to combine. You want to mix the batter until just smooth. Add the rum and briefly whisk until combined. Dollop the batter evenly over the caramel and pineapple layers in the cake tin, using a small spatula to smooth over.

6. Bake for 30–35 minutes until a skewer comes out clean. Leave to cool in the tin for 5 minutes, then place a plate on top and flip it over in one swift movement. The cake should come clean out of the tin. Serve warm.

TIP

When cooking fruit in caramel, I wear a pair of (clean) washing up gloves to protect my hands and arms.

pie dough

Makes enough for 1 pie or galette

Pie dough is very rewarding to make, not to mention head and shoulders above anything you could buy. I am indebted to Nicola Lamb for the technique here and I will repeat her advice, too: the key when making pie dough is not to panic, okay? It will seem too dry and a bit of a craggy mess at first, but it will all come together after a few folds and a good rest in the fridge (minimum 4 hours, but ideally overnight). Trust the process.

1.   In a small jug, whisk together the water and sour cream, then place in the fridge.

2.   In a medium bowl, whisk together the flour, sugar and salt. Add the butter and toss to coat (this helps to protect the butter from the warmth of your hands). Squish the butter into flat pieces, one by one.

3.   Pour in the cold sour cream mixture and squish the dough together with your hands. As soon as it's vaguely coming together (it will still be quite dry and chaotic), tip the dough onto your work surface and squash everything together as best you can. You can add another tablespoon of water here, if you really need to, but this pastry should remain on the dry side – keep the faith.

4.   Roll out the dough, adding flour if you need to, and perform a single turn. You'll see the chunks of butter start to turn into long, thin pieces.

5.   Roll the dough into a long rectangle (it should be 2–3 times longer than it is wide), then use the dough scraper (or the side of the rolling pin) to nudge the pastry back into a neat shape. Place any dry bits that won't stick into the middle of the rectangle. Ease the dough scraper under the top third of the rectangle of pastry and flip it over into the middle. Use the dough scraper to fold the remaining bottom third of the pastry over the top of the already folded section so that you have a neat rectangular block comprised of three layers. This process is called a 'single turn'.

6.   Turn the dough 90 degrees and repeat the above process, performing two more 'single turns' (three single turns in total). The dough should become more homogenous as you do this, and you'll see streaks of butter start to develop in the dough, like marble.

7.   Wrap the dough in cling film (plastic wrap) and place in the fridge for at least 4 hours (or overnight) to firm up.

60ml (2fl oz/¼ cup) ice-cold water, plus extra as needed
60ml (2fl oz/¼ cup) sour cream
250g (9oz/2 cups) plain (all-purpose) flour, plus extra for rolling out, if needed
25g (1oz/2 tbsp) caster (superfine) sugar
1 tsp flaky sea salt
185g (6½oz) butter, fridge-cold and cut into 1.5cm (¾in) cubes

equipment
dough scraper (helpful, but not essential)

TIP
A dough scraper is a multi-tasking hero in the kitchen. Not only is it useful when working with doughs, but it also enables you to transport large quantities of prepped veg from cutting board to pan, and is useful for cleaning your surfaces once you've finished cooking.

index

BIBLIOGRAPHY

Amedi, Tomer, and Paskin, Layo, *The Palomar Cookbook*, Mitchell Beazley, 2016

Balch, Oliver, 'Mars, Nestlé and Hershey to Face Child Slavery Lawsuit in US', *Guardian*, February 12, 2021

Berger, Miriam, 'Is the World Ready for this Palestinian Dish?', BBC.com, March 28, 2019

Berman-Vaporis, Irene, Elliott, Kennedy, and Wardley, Rosemary, 'The U.S. Cranberry Harvest Explained in Four Charts', *National Geographic*, November 27, 2019

Blakemore, Erin, 'Chocolate Gets Its Sweet History Rewritten', *National Geographic*, November 2, 2018

'Cranberries: No Longer Just an American Tradition', Foreign Agricultural Service, US Department of Agriculture, November 22, 2016

De La Fuente Del Moral, Fatima, 'How Europe Went Crazy for Cocoa', *National Geographic*, November 16, 2018

Doucleff, Michaeleen, 'Why Can We Taste Bitter Flavors? Turns Out, It's Still a Mystery', NPR.org, November 13, 2013

Druse, Ken, 'The Cranberry Is Not Just for Sauce', *New York Times*, December 25, 2003

Furseth, Jessica, 'Everything You Always Wanted to Know About Licorice', Eater.com, August 24, 2021

'How Coffee Shops Brewed Up a Revolution', Folklore Series, Eater.com, August 29, 2016

Kral, Linni, 'Why Is Iceland So in Love with Licorice?', *Gastro Obscura*, April 24, 2017

Larousse Gastronomique, Hamlyn, 2009

MacEacheran, Mike, 'The Strange Story of Britain's Oldest Sweet', BBC.com, July 11, 2019

McGee, Harold, *On Food and Cooking: The Science and Lore of the Kitchen*, Hodder & Stoughton, 2004

McHugo, John, 'Coffee and Qahwa: How a Drink for Arab Mystics Went Global', BBC.com, April 18, 2013

McLagan, Jennifer, *Bitter: A Taste of the World's Most Dangerous Flavor*, Ten Speed Press, 2014

Nosowitz, Dan, 'Grapefruit Is One of the Weirdest Fruits on the Planet', *Atlas Obscura*, October 6, 2020

Nosrat, Samin, *Salt Fat Acid Heat*, Canongate, 2017

Park, Michael Y., 'How Our Sense of Taste Changes as We Age', *Bon Appétit*, March 14, 2014

Pendergast, Mark, *Uncommon Grounds: The History of Coffee and How It Transformed Our World*, Basic Books, 2019 (new edition)

Phillips, Rod, 'A Brief History of Alcohol', YouTube, January 2, 2020

Pinnock, Dale, *The Medicinal Chef*, Quadrille, 2013

Pollan, Michael, *This Is Your Mind on Plants*, Penguin, 2021

Pucciarelli, Deanna (via TED-Ed), 'The History of Chocolate', YouTube, March 16, 2017

Quinn, Sue, *Cocoa*, Quadrille/Hardie Grant Publishing, 2019

Randell, Sarah, *Marmalade: A Bittersweet Cookbook*, Headline Home, 2014

Rapp Learn, Joshua, 'The Maya Civilisation Used Chocolate as Money', Science.org, June 27, 2018

Rochlin, Margy, 'This Pastry Chef Didn't Like Liquorice – Until She Became Obsessed with It', *Los Angeles Times*, July 13, 2018

Rupp, Rebecca, 'Walnuts Through Time: Brain Food, Poison, Money, Muse', *National Geographic*, September 29, 2015

Saladino, Dan, *The Food Programme*, 'Bitterness', BBC Radio 4, October 5, 2015

Scott, Aaron, Grayeson, Gisele, and Tesfay, Eva, 'TASTE BUDDIES: The Controversial World of Taste Science', NPR.org, August 1, 2022

Scott, Aaron, and McCoy, Berly, 'TASTE BUDDIES: Why Bitter Tastes Better for Some', NPR.org, May 19, 2022

Segnit, Niki, *The Flavour Thesaurus: Pairings, Recipes and Ideas for the Creative Cook*, Bloomsbury, 2010

Slave Free Chocolate Coalition, www.slavefreechocolate.org

Teng, Shunan (via TED-Ed), 'The History of Tea', YouTube, May 16, 2017

Wilson, Carol, *Liquorice: A Cookbook*, Lorenz Books, 2018

Zaraska, Marta, 'Bitter Truth: How We're Making Fruit and Veg Less Healthy', *New Scientist*, July 29, 2015

THANK YOU

Wow, I could have never predicted how much of a rollercoaster the last couple of years would be. Some real ones have helped me through.

To my sisters, **Jade** and **Asha**. Lord knows there have been tears, and laughter, and moments of tough love. I appreciate you more than you know.

To my girls – **Katie, Anais, Charissa, Robyn, Minnie, Rea** – thank you for the unwavering support over the years, from near and far. Thank you also to **Ian** and **Grace** – we don't get to see each other as much as I'd like (still annoyed you didn't move south of the river . . .) but it's always a good time when we do, and I have appreciated your support in key moments (including vase-gate . . .).

To the many others in my life, who have helped me along this journey in all sorts of ways – **Jay, Byron, Jordan, Richard, Alice, Octavia, Matthew, Sonia, Rosaria, Marcus, Vivi** and **Henry** – thank you.

To the creative team – **Yuki, Lola, Lucie, Evi O, Georgia, Caitlin, Nora, Julyan** – thank you for putting together such a beautiful book, I'm in awe of your talents. I also acknowledge that I'm picky as hell, so thank you for indulging me.

To the editorial team – **Marianne** and **Emily**, I cannot thank you enough for the time, energy and love that you have brought to this project. Thank you for always being in my corner.

To **Mireille**, my commissioning editor – thank you for seeing the potential in this series, and in me . . . you made it happen!

To **Hannah Telfer**, thank you for your time and passion on this project, even as you run the whole of Vintage (no big deal . . .). It's been inspiring to work with you.

My deepest thanks to the rest of the **Square Peg team**, as well as **Emily Preece-Morrison**, who have been so passionate about this project from the beginning and have offered so much support – I am very grateful!

The biggest thank you to my agent, **Milly Reilly**: from our first meeting I knew you were 'the one' and I've never ever regretted that decision. Thank you for being my biggest supporter.

To those who contributed to the book – including Charlotte Cook for teaching me all about beer – or have generally inspired me in the food space – thank you.

To **all those who have come to my supper clubs**, including my regulars, it has meant more than you know. And thank you to all my Instagram **followers**, too. You've been a lovely, supportive bunch – and very patient with my supremely inconsistent online presence!

To my *MasterChef* **family** – Kerry, Mike, Josh, Jim, Claire, Mike, Laura, Rishi – so glad the show brought us together. And thank you to the entire *MasterChef* **production team** for giving me a platform to launch from.

Thank you to **Liz** and the **Saint Lucia Tourism Authority** for your support over the last year, and for helping me to reconnect to my roots.

To **Roy**, thank you for believing in me and all that you've invested into this crazy journey. I am in awe of what you've done, and I hope to learn a lot from you as we continue on this adventure. And to **Anais** (again), for trusting us – we love you.

Thank you to **Stu** – who knew this crazy journey was going to lead me to you? I so value our friendship, chats about the world and, of course, cocktail hour (it has to be a Negroni, doesn't it?).

Thank you to **Miss P** for teaching me so much about food – you will forever be a culinary inspiration to me.

Thank you to **Robert** (and, by extension, his lovely family) for taking me under your cultural wing all those years ago and helping me feel like I belonged. I miss you.

To those I've not named here, but who have been part of my journey at some point along the way, and have believed in me, thank you.

And finally, my family. **Dad** and **Julia** – for always supporting me. **Matthew** – I love you! Peter – thank you for always being there to help, with tasks big and small. **Gran** and **Grandpa** – thank you for creating the best childhood memories. All those summers and Christmases spent at the farm are some of my most treasured times. Thank you for always supporting me – I hope to continue to make you proud.

Above all else, **Mum** – thank you for everything you've done for me since the day I was born. Your wisdom, intelligence, care and love are everything. My success is your success and I'd truly be lost without you.

1 3 5 7 9 10 8 6 4 2

Square Peg, an imprint of Vintage,
is part of the Penguin Random House group of
companies whose addresses can be found at
global.penguinrandomhouse.com

Penguin
Random House
UK

First published by Square Peg in 2023

Book Designer: Lucie, Studio 7:15

Cover Designer: Evi-O.Studio

Food Photographer: Yuki Sugiura

Food Photography Assistant: Nora Pribek

Food Stylist: Lola Milne

Food Styling Assistants: Georgia Rudd and Caitlin
Macdonald

Portrait Photographer: Danika Magdelena

Prop Stylist: Susie Clegg

penguin.co.uk/vintage

Printed and bound in China by C&C Offset Printing Co., Ltd.

The authorised representative in the EEA is Penguin
Random House Ireland, Morrison Chambers, 32 Nassau
Street, Dublin D02 YH68

A CIP catalogue record for this book is available from the
British Library

ISBN 9781529193121

Penguin Random House is committed to a sustainable future for
our business, our readers and our planet. This book is made from
Forest Stewardship Council® certified paper.

MIX
Paper | Supporting
responsible forestry
FSC® C018179

Alexina is a cook who researches, writes and talks
about flavour: the science of it, how it appears
across different cultures (she is herself mixed race)
and how to translate this into delicious food in
the kitchen. Alexina was a finalist on *MasterChef*
2021 where she demonstrated her enthusiasm for
grapefruit, love of liquorice and intense dislike
of mint chocolate. *Bitter*, published by Vintage,
Penguin Random House, is her debut cookbook
and the first in a series centred around the five
tastes (bitter, sweet, sour, salty and umami).

www.alexinaanatole.com